Teacher Leaders,

CLASSROOM CHAMPIONS

*How to Influence, Support, and Renew
School Communities*

JEANETTA JONES MILLER

Solution Tree | Press
a division of
Solution Tree

555 North Morton Street
Bloomington, IN 47404
800.733.6786 (toll free) / 812.336.7700
FAX: 812.336.7790

email: info@SolutionTree.com
SolutionTree.com

Visit **go.SolutionTree.com/teacherefficacy** to download the free reproducibles in this book.

Printed in the United States of America

Library of Congress Cataloging-in-Publication Data

Names: Miller, Jeanetta Jones, author.

Title: Teacher leaders, classroom champions : how to influence, support, and renew school communities / Jeanetta Jones Miller.

Description: Bloomington, IN : Solution Tree Press, 2023. | Includes bibliographical references and index.

Identifiers: LCCN 2022045833 (print) | LCCN 2022045834 (ebook) | ISBN 9781954631892 (paperback) | ISBN 9781954631908 (ebook)

Subjects: LCSH: Teachers--Professional relationships. | Educational leadership. | Effective teaching. | Reflective teaching. | Educational accountability. | Teacher-student relationships. | Parent-teacher relationships.

Classification: LCC LB1775 .M616 2023 (print) | LCC LB1775 (ebook) | DDC 371.1--dc23/eng/20221116

LC record available at https://lccn.loc.gov/2022045833

LC ebook record available at https://lccn.loc.gov/2022045834

Solution Tree
Jeffrey C. Jones, CEO
Edmund M. Ackerman, President

Solution Tree Press
President and Publisher: Douglas M. Rife
Associate Publisher: Sarah Payne-Mills
Managing Production Editor: Kendra Slayton
Editorial Director: Todd Brakke
Art Director: Rian Anderson
Copy Chief: Jessi Finn
Production Editor: Miranda Addonizio
Content Development Specialist: Amy Rubenstein
Copy Editor: Jessi Finn
Proofreader: Charlotte Jones
Text and Cover Designer: Julie Csizmadia
Associate Editor: Sarah Ludwig
Editorial Assistant: Elijah Oates

ACKNOWLEDGMENTS

When I look back, it seems as if there were always people right there ready to inform, encourage, and inspire me to do what I could to make learning meaningful, even joyful, for my students. These were the teacher leaders, looking out for those new to the profession, providing support for colleagues, and contributing tirelessly to improving instruction and student learning. I'm indebted to the presenters at the Bay Area Writing Project and at Bard College's Institute for Writing and Thinking who shared ideas and strategies—teacher to teacher—that helped me make English class feel like a "get to" instead of a "have to" for students. I'm indebted to colleagues in Newtown Public Schools who launched cross-grade and multidisciplinary initiatives that got me out of my own building to explore what education looks like from the perspectives of elementary and middle schools and the district office. And I am especially indebted to my colleagues in the English department at Newtown High School who inspired me to strive to be a better teacher and, as time passed, to be a teacher leader they could count on.

When the time came to become a teacher leader, and it seemed that every day brought a new challenge, I often turned to my husband, Charles Miller, for support and encouragement. I also turned to him as the ideas and structure for this book began to take shape. He is a good listener, has a knack for making apt comments, and is always ready to commiserate or celebrate.

I would like to add my thanks to the reviewers for challenging me to rethink and rewrite and encouraging me to make this a book that supports and celebrates leadership that originates in and is sustained by what teachers do every day in the classroom. I would also like to thank Miranda Addonizio for her insightful and incisive work as the production editor of this book, as well as the many members of the Solution Tree team whose collaborative efforts have resulted in *Teacher Leaders, Classroom Champions*. I am awed and grateful.

Solution Tree Press would like to thank the following reviewers:

Johanna Josaphat
Teacher-Leader
The Urban Assembly Unison School
Brooklyn, New York

Amy Kochensparger
High School Science Teacher, Science
Department Chair
Eaton High School
Eaton, Ohio

Josh Kunnath
High School English Teacher, Grading
& Assessment Consultant
Kern High School District
Bakersfield, California

Shanna Martin
Middle School Teacher & Instructional
Coach
School District of Lomira
Lomira, Wisconsin

Nicole McRee
Science Instructional Coach
Kildeer Countryside District 96
Buffalo Grove, Illinois

Tara Reed
Fourth-Grade Language Arts and
Curriculum Writer
Denton ISD
Denton, Texas

Visit **go.SolutionTree.com/teacherefficacy** to download the free reproducibles in this book.

TABLE OF CONTENTS

Reproducibles are in italics.

About the Author . . . . **ix**

Introduction **1**

CHAPTER 1

**A Closer Look at
Teacher Leadership** **5**

Teacher Leader Responsibilities. 5

Teacher Leaders in Action 6

Summary 11

Next Steps for a Closer Look at Teacher Leadership 12

CHAPTER 2

A Collaborative and Connected Culture **15**

Classroom Collaboration 16

Collegial Safety Net. 20

Collaborative Meetings 28

A Connected School Community. 30

Schoolwide Planning 31

Connections With Families 33

Summary 38

Lesson-Planning Chart 39

Next Steps for a Collaborative and Connected Culture. 40

CHAPTER 3

Research and Professional Learning to Meet Student Needs **43**

Classroom Action Research 44

Collect Information and Develop a Plan 45

Implement the Plan and Evaluate the Results 48

Repeat the Process 51

Demonstration Lessons 54

Summary 57

Next Steps for Research and Professional Learning to Meet Student Needs 59

CHAPTER 4

Renewal and Improvement of Instruction and Student Learning **61**

Teacher-Written Curriculum 62

Elements of an Effective Curriculum 62

The Case for Follow-Up 68

Student Feedback 70

Assessments That Help and Encourage Students 73

Teacher Observation and Read-Back of Student Activities 74

Sampling of Class Responses to an Activity 74

Preference Surveys 75

Progress Logs 76

Student Self-Assessment and Reflection 76

Student-Teacher and Peer Conferences 77

Problem Solving 79

Summary 80

Curriculum-Writing Guidelines 81

Next Steps for Renewal and Improvement of Instruction and Student Learning 82

Conclusion: Advocates in the Classroom. 85

References and Resources. 87

Index 93

ABOUT THE AUTHOR

 *Jeanetta Jones Miller* has been an educator since 1986. Her education experiences include working with continuation high school students in a voluntary diploma program, integrating all subject areas with fifth graders, and developing a student-centered approach in high school. She has taught American studies and senior projects as well as a variety of English courses. Miller served as department chair at Newtown High School in Sandy Hook, Connecticut, and mentored many teachers with a consistent focus on research, development, and implementation of strategies that help all students engage deeply in learning.

Miller has participated in a number of organizations related to her teaching and leadership goals, including the National Council of Teachers of English (NCTE) and the Bay Area and Connecticut Writing Projects. She served on district committees that studied graduation standards, K–12 language arts, and aspects of learning such as reflection and self-direction. She was a lead writer for Newtown High School's successful application for recognition as a U.S. Department of Education Blue Ribbon School in 2000. In 2010 she won NCTE's English Language Arts Teacher Educators (ELATE) James Moffett Memorial Award for Teacher Research.

With two colleagues, she wrote *High Stakes High School*, a publication intended to help families navigate standardized testing. Miller's conviction is that individual classroom teachers can combine teaching and leadership to foster a collaborative culture that benefits students, educators, and families. She has also written about the benefits of a student-centered approach in the classroom. She initially developed these ideas in an article for *English Journal* and further developed them in 2021 when writing *The Student-Centered Classroom*; both of these serve as resources for professional learning.

Miller earned a bachelor's degree from Mills College and qualified for multiple-subject and single-subject teaching credentials at California State University, East

Bay. She earned a master's degree in education focused on curriculum from Western Connecticut State University and an intermediate administrator's certificate from Sacred Heart University.

To book Jeanetta Jones Miller for professional development, contact pd@SolutionTree.com.

Introduction

There's an old saying: if you want to get something done, you should ask a busy person. Classroom teachers who take the time and make the effort to get to know students, support colleagues, and contribute to a collaborative school community are, indeed, busy people. The day-to-day work of these classroom champions has a positive influence within and beyond the classroom. Such teacher leaders' work is never done because it generates a continuous cycle of learning and innovation that renews the school community and returns to the classroom for new learning and innovation.

Ask, "When is a good time to be a teacher leader?" and the answer will be, "Now." Ask, "Where is a good place to be a teacher leader?" and the answer will be, "Where you are." Ask, "What is a good reason to be a teacher leader?" and the answer will be, "Influence, support, and renewal." Ask, "How do I become a teacher leader?" and the answer will be, "Keep asking." Teacher leadership can inspire and support colleagues at all levels of experience, engage families, contribute to a collaborative school climate, and have a lasting impact on the lives of students.

Educators who serve as both teachers and leaders are referred to as *teacher leaders* most of the time; sometimes you'll see this role hyphenated. Sylvia S. Bagley (2016), director of teacher leadership at the University of Washington, speaks for the hyphenators in her commentary for *Teachers College Record*:

> Just like we refer to a military leader as a leader of the military, a business leader as a leader of a business, a government leader as a leader of a government, a school leader as a leader of a school, and a religious leader as a leader of a religious group, a teacher leader would most likely be parsed as a leader of teachers. (p. 1)

Teacher leaders, however, do not lead teachers. That responsibility resides with administrators. Bagley (2016), who prefers the term *teacher-leader*, cites a meta-review of research on what these professionals actually do. The domains include "coordinating, managing, mentoring, coaching, developing curriculum, conducting research, facilitating workshops, participating in school improvement initiatives, and becoming involved in parent and community efforts," but there is no mention of *leading* (Bagley, 2016, pp. 1–2). While I find Bagley's (2016) reasoning sound, I think it's fair to say that the term *teacher leader* appropriately captures the dual role these classroom champions play. It's important to be clear that teacher leaders are not administrators, but teacher leaders do influence, guide, and lead colleagues by example and by formal and informal coaching and mentorship. They take on a variety of responsibilities that support teachers, improve student learning, inform and involve families, and contribute to a positive school climate.

Teacher leadership is not a new concept, and it has been written about before. But just picking up a book about teacher leadership is a hit-or-miss prospect because resources often concentrate on classic leadership skills geared toward positional leaders rather than the much narrower and subtler definition I explore here. My definition of teacher leadership might be narrower; however, it's far broader than that of teacher leadership in the sense of a school leader, because my definition means any teacher can lead in this way.

Teacher leaders can make incremental but significant improvements in classrooms, across grade levels, and in content areas that are eye opening and life altering for both colleagues and students. Getting what's going on in school to align with what's good for students may involve trying something new, modifying current practice, or stopping a practice that does not contribute to student learning. Real change doesn't happen overnight, and schoolwide change requires a sustained collaborative effort. But teacher leaders are flexible and can act quickly to understand and resolve an issue.

Let's say you're a teacher leader, and you've noticed something that could use improvement in your own teaching practice. You don't want to make changes without some confidence that the results will be good for student learning. You start by developing a survey and studying students' responses. Then you do some background research to learn what other educators have done in similar situations. You share what you're learning with a colleague or two and decide to work as a team. You try a small adjustment first, and when that works, you try something bigger. You're clear about the results you're hoping for and patient about seeing those results appear. I would guess that, before too long, you'd know your classroom experimentation is good for students because you see their eyes light up as their sense of belonging and their engagement in learning increase. Then you might want to let families know how things are going and share what you've done with more colleagues so they can try it.

There are, of course, infinite variations on this scenario. Its purpose is not to set forth a series of steps that you must take but to offer a sketch of teacher leadership in action. Teacher leadership's positive impact on student learning and school culture is at the core of the National Education Association's (NEA, 2020) Teacher Leader Model Standards. As you read through the seven domains, you'll see that the steps suggested in the sketch address most of them:

- **Domain I:** Fostering a collaborative culture to support educator development and student learning

- **Domain II:** Accessing and using research to improve practice and student learning

- **Domain III:** Promoting professional learning for continuous improvement

- **Domain IV:** Facilitating improvements in instruction and student learning

- **Domain V:** Promoting the use of assessments and data for school and district improvement

- **Domain VI:** Improving outreach and collaboration with families and community

- **Domain VII:** Advocating for student learning and the profession (NEA, 2020)

As advocates and activists for student learning and the profession (domain VII), teacher leaders do not have to wait for a new initiative or practice to come from or be directed by an administrator; they can initiate change from the classroom. A teacher leader from Brooklyn, New York, puts it this way: "A teacher in a classroom has the ability to impact the learning that happens for their students using the instruction they deliver every day. A strong, well-trained teacher leader can shift practice for a school community" (J. Josaphat, personal communication, June 16, 2022).

This book draws from all seven domains of the Teacher Leader Model Standards (NEA, 2020). From them, I chose to focus on three overarching aspects: (1) collaboration and connection, (2) research and professional learning, and (3) renewal and improvement of instruction and student learning.

Chapter 1 goes into depth to clarify exactly what teacher leadership is, what effective teacher leaders do, and what traits teacher leaders can work on developing. Chapters 2–4 focus on each of the three aspects described previously.

Chapter 2 explores how teacher leaders contribute to a collaborative culture by supporting and encouraging colleagues, both in and out of the classroom. Teacher leaders do this by building competence and confidence in those new to the profession, spearheading schoolwide collaborative planning, and connecting with students and families.

Chapter 3 focuses on the research and innovation teacher leaders engage in to develop effective materials and methods. This work is crucial to students' success both in school and in the larger world.

Chapter 4 addresses the vital process of renewing instruction to meet changing times and changing student needs. The chapter includes discussion of teacher-generated curriculum work, follow-up, and student feedback, and it also provides some insight on using assessments as tools to improve instruction and student outcomes. In my experience, the best outcomes occur in classrooms and among colleagues who work to support one another and meet specific student needs.

At the end of each chapter is a reproducible tool that lists some suggested next steps and provides space to reflect (and add your own next steps).

The conclusion provides information about the methods teacher leaders use to advocate for student learning and the profession of teaching.

Like the teacher leader's dual role, this book has a dual purpose: (1) to recognize the contributions teacher leaders make every day to support colleagues and improve student learning and (2) to open doors for teachers who are ready to activate learning from the classroom and step into that dual role of teacher leader themselves.

CHAPTER 1

A Closer Look at Teacher Leadership

Teaching is multifaceted. Teachers meet the needs of many people, which is inevitably taxing, so they need sources of renewal. Strong coffee and long walks can help, but the most effective source of renewal I've found is serving as a teacher leader. Just like students, teachers need a sense of belonging. Taking time to really listen to a new teacher, participating in an exchange of demonstration lessons, working with colleagues on a research project, joining a committee or getting involved in organizing an event, reaching out to families—all these things take time, but the sense of connection and the affirmation of who you are that they foster are worth it.

But *what* do teacher leaders actually do? And what types of actions might they cultivate to be successful? This chapter answers those questions.

TEACHER LEADER RESPONSIBILITIES

There are many ways of trying on teacher leadership to see whether it's a good fit.

The definition of *teacher leader* developed for *The Glossary of Education Reform* (2014) by the Great Schools Partnership provides a substantial list of possible teacher leader responsibilities; the following summary provides some highlights.

- **Serve on a team:** You could serve on anything from a leadership team to a collaborative content-area or grade-level team, a committee assigned to improve schoolwide or content-area curriculum, or a school or district task force assigned to spearhead a particular school-improvement program.

- **Mentor or otherwise support colleagues:** Train or supervise new teachers; take on the role of a learning facilitator or instructional coach to help all teachers with instruction, classroom management, data collection and analysis, skill building with technology, and so on; or model innovative strategies for other teachers.
- **Share knowledge and skills:** There are countless ways to do this, including making videos, hosting online discussion forums, developing webinars, speaking at professional conferences or meetings, and writing for professional publications.
- **Liaise with students, families, and the school community:** This could include finding ways to let students work together to improve their schools, districts, and communities. Help families engage in what's going on at school. You could also work with local businesses or community organizations to provide opportunities for students.
- **Become an advocate:** This could involve getting into local, state or provincial, or national advocacy groups that aim to educate students and make their lives better; fundraising for school or district programs; or making your voice heard by contacting elected officials or testifying in public hearings.

There are as many ways to be a teacher leader as there are teachers willing to take on this dual role. Sometimes being a teacher leader is just a matter of being willing. Sometimes an opportunity arises from a professional learning activity or a school event. Sometimes training or coursework is required. Occasionally, there might be an application to fill out and a review process to undergo. For the most part, if you want to step up, you will be welcomed. Many of the possible teacher leader responsibilities focus on achieving a specific goal or serving for a specific period of time. When the goal or term has been fulfilled, you're done. But I hope you find the dual role of teacher leader so stimulating and rewarding that being a teacher leader becomes an essential part of who you are as an educator.

TEACHER LEADERS IN ACTION

As you may have surmised from the range of responsibilities outlined in the previous section, there is no single profile of a teacher leader. Tiffany Perry (2022) is a fifth-grade teacher in Florida who has been trying new strategies with her students, even though some of those strategies take her outside of her comfort zone.

Sharing authority in the classroom with students is very hard for a teacher to do, yet Perry (2022) decided to do it when she was certain her students would benefit from increased opportunities to make decisions and shoulder responsibility for the quality of their own educational experience. She explains:

> On the first day of school . . . , I gave my class directions for our activity and told them, "I need five groups." They looked at me for a few seconds; and then, when they realized I wasn't going to say anything else, a few students started counting how many people were in class and moving them into groups. At that moment, my students could tell that I wasn't always going to tell them exactly what to do and that they could make decisions on their own. (Perry, 2022)

Perry also experimented with the Socratic seminars that she didn't experience until high school, but which became her fifth graders' favorite activity. She writes, "I quickly realized how much they were capable of when I didn't try to rescue them and just sat quietly on the side" (Perry, 2022). Another venture into new territory was embarking on coding with a borrowed set of Sphero robots. Perry (2022) had little experience with these robots, but she says, "I didn't want to let my inexperience and nervousness keep my students from this learning opportunity." Working in teams, the class practiced coding the robots until first one team and then all the teams were able to get their Spheros through a zigzag course. Both students and teacher grew as coders, risk takers, and problem solvers.

Teague Tubach (2022) is a middle school teacher leader in California who shared his family's outreach to unhoused people with his students, initiating a project-based learning experience that was life changing for everyone involved. The project "would emphasize critical thinking and compassion and include research, argumentative writing, multivoice poetry, a service-learning component, and the creation of an interactive experience for [the] community" (Tubach, 2022).

Some of Tubach's (2022) students had experienced homelessness, and all of them had witnessed it, but it seemed as if little had been done about it. They were motivated to learn more through research, to make tangible contributions through local food kitchens and the creation and distribution of hundreds of personal hygiene kits, and to make the suffering of unhoused people visible with a public art project. Reflecting on the experience, Tubach (2022) writes:

> Shadows still exist in our society, but that doesn't mean that our unhoused neighbors are invisible. When students use project-based learning to take a deep dive into a real-world issue with an emphasis on critical thinking and compassion, they can strengthen their community and radiate real change.

Although their profiles differ, Tiffany Perry and Teague Tubach both engage in deliberate actions that teacher leaders tend to have in common. These are not instinctive skills that some people are born with and others just have to do without. Actions such as those reflected on by Perry and Tubach are likely already evident in your teaching practice. Once you are aware of specific actions you use to support and improve student learning and the role those actions play in teacher leadership, you can consciously expand your capacity to contribute to the success of both students and colleagues. Knowing why your approach to teaching works for students and being able to share that knowledge with colleagues are right at the core of teacher leadership.

A study of research on what makes a teacher highly effective identifies eight types of deliberate action engaged in by teachers who "refine their practices, improve their craft, and make a significant—or even life-altering—contribution to the lives of their students" (Terada & Merrill, 2022). The eight types of action focus on what happens in the classroom. The following list adds a ninth type of action related to activism beyond the classroom.

1. **Willingness to solicit feedback:** Ask students for feedback and use what you learn to improve your teaching. Tubach (2022), for example, sets up the project for his students so that it provides him with continuous feedback about the project's impact on the students as well as the students' impact on the community.

2. **Enthusiasm for connection and collaboration:** Meet students' need to be connected with other students through collaborative work and opportunities to bring their lives into the classroom. Perry (2022) carefully observes her students before, while, and after saying, "I need five groups." From these observations, she determines that "they could make decisions on their own" (Perry, 2022).

3. **Tolerance for challenge and risk:** Provide challenging—sometimes messy—assignments, and expect risk taking, failure, revision, and deep learning. Because she wants her students to experience coding and knows they will benefit whether the activity succeeds or fails, Perry (2022) accepts the risk of introducing an activity that is challenging for her as well as her students.

4. **Readiness to earn respect:** Make classroom management invisible by earning the respect of students. Both Perry (2022) and Tubach (2022)

do this by expecting a lot from their students and appreciating the positive impact they have on the classroom community and on the larger community.

5. **Anticipation of engagement in learning:** Maintain high standards and take a user-friendly approach, emphasizing learning over grades. Even though they teach in quite different settings, Perry (2022) and Tubach (2022) have similar goals in that they both want their students to engage deeply in learning.

6. **Fidelity to student perspectives:** Focus on learning goals that include students in the assessment process and help you avoid inadvertent bias. Whether having students move into five groups or work for social justice, Perry (2022) and Tubach (2022) set things up so their students can demonstrate progress in important areas such as collaboration and problem solving.

7. **Desire to share and generate lifelong learning:** Earn trust by being yourself, sharing your passions, and doing the background work necessary to broaden and deepen your understanding. Introducing the Socratic seminar so it becomes the favorite activity of fifth graders and making it possible for middle school students to engage safely yet impactfully with real community issues require long hours of homework from Perry (2022) and Tubach (2022). But that work makes it possible for them to share their own passions with students, making life richer for both students and teachers.

8. **Attention to balance between rigor and ease:** Shift focus so teaching time is balanced with time for rest and recreation. While Perry's (2022) and Tubach's (2022) students surely spend some time seated at desks or tables working on pencil-and-paper tasks, their teachers highlight times when students are up and about and even outside the school building. Variations in focus and location are refreshing, which is why I taught my students the yoga-based tree pose as a way to get them up and refocused even in a high school classroom packed with desk-chair units.

9. **Commitment to advocacy:** Advocate for the profession of teaching and for student learning. I learned about what goes on in Perry's (2022) and Tubach's (2022) classes from the articles they wrote for Edutopia. Writing an article is one of many ways teachers can share

strategies and insights that promote broader understanding of what effective teaching looks like and deeper understanding of what active student learning looks like. This book's conclusion on page 85 discusses advocacy in a little more detail.

The chart in figure 1.1 provides an opportunity to reflect on the degree to which these nine types of action align with your practice or goals as a teacher leader.

Actions of Teacher Leaders	Alignment With Your Practice		
	Total	Partial	Not so much
Ask students for feedback and use what you learn to improve your teaching.			
Meet students' need to be connected with other students through collaborative work and opportunities to bring their lives into the classroom.			
Provide challenging—sometimes messy—assignments, and expect risk taking, failure, revision, and deep learning.			
Make classroom management "invisible" by earning the respect of students.			
Maintain high standards and take a user-friendly approach, emphasizing learning over grades.			
Focus on learning goals that include students in the assessment process and help you avoid inadvertent bias.			
Earn trust by being yourself, sharing your passions, and doing the background work necessary to broaden and deepen your understanding.			
Shift focus so teaching time is balanced with time for rest and recreation.			
Advocate for the profession of teaching and for student learning.			

Source: Terada & Merrill, 2022.

FIGURE 1.1: Chart for rating alignment of teacher leader actions and your own practice.

Visit **go.SolutionTree.com/teacherefficacy** for a free reproducible version of this figure.

SUMMARY

As a teacher leader, you try new things and make informed decisions about what works best for students. This continuous process helps you understand not only how a teaching strategy works but also why it works. Awareness of both how and why gives a teacher leader much to share with colleagues.

The responsibilities that teacher leaders may take on are just as varied as the teachers who strive to fulfill them. It is my hope that all teachers will find within these possibilities a niche where they can truly make a difference in and from the classroom. The actions that teacher leaders can take likewise reflect attributes that any teacher can work to develop. As you reflect on how your classroom practices align with these actions, consider how you might further progress. A good way to start is with the next steps on page 12, a reproducible tool that suggests some ways forward and provides space to envision your own. When you're ready, the next chapter discusses the ways in which collaboration and connection within classrooms, among teachers, and with the whole school community can further learning outcomes for all students.

NEXT STEPS FOR A CLOSER LOOK AT TEACHER LEADERSHIP

The following tool details some steps you can take to experiment with strategies for activating leadership from the classroom. For each step, note the date you tried it and reflect on how it went. *What did you do? How did it go? What would you change? What's next?* There are spaces available at the end for you to plan additional steps you can take toward teacher leadership.

Next Steps Tried	Date Tried	Reflection
Take a look at the summary of teacher leader responsibilities on pages 5–6, and make a list of those you've already tried; then, add one more you'd like to try.		
Use the reproducible version of figure 1.1 (page 10) to rate your use of such teacher leader actions in your teaching practice.		
Identify one action taken by Tiffany Perry (2022) or Teague Tubach (2022) that appeals to you but might entail a bit of risk, and figure out a way to try something like it with your students.		

Gather feedback from your students about your action experiment through observation, a quick survey, a sampling of student responses, or a combination.		

References

Perry, T. (2022, June 8). Promoting student-led learning in elementary school. Accessed at www.edutopia.org/article/promoting-student-led-learning-elementary-school on June 26, 2022.

Tubach, T. (2022, June 15). Using PBL to teach about homelessness. Accessed at www.edutopia.org/article/using-pbl-teach-about-homelessness on June 26, 2022.

CHAPTER 2

A Collaborative and Connected Culture

Culture is the sum of what any given group values and what distinguishes one group from another. What is valued in school culture has evolved from managing classrooms like a factory assembly line to creating classrooms where students are appreciated as individuals (Darling-Hammond & Cook-Harvey, 2018). Educators have learned that students thrive when they have opportunities to collaborate with other students and when they feel connected with the school as a whole (Surr, Zeiser, Briggs, & Kendziora, 2018). The collaborative and connected culture that helps students thrive also helps teachers thrive (Azorín & Fullan, 2022). In such a culture, teachers have support and encouragement to try new things, share with colleagues, and take on the dual role of teaching and leadership.

You can feel the positive impact of a collaborative and connected school culture like a morning breeze wafting through school hallways, making the whole building feel alive with possibility. Such a culture is never perfect, never done, but working toward a collaborative, connected culture creates an environment in which all members of a school community can realize their full potential. I might park my car and walk toward the school entrance with a little tension headache from checking my to-do list and wondering what I have forgotten. But the headache vanishes as I get caught up in the energy generated within the school building. Educating all students—*all* the children of *all* the people—is a daunting task, but working with an entire school community to achieve this goal can be exhilarating.

Some collaborative work is formal, such as organizing a professional learning team at the building level or participating in a committee to study a district initiative's impact on student learning. But much of the collaborative work in which teacher leaders engage is informal, generated in the moment to help classroom teachers meet student needs, such as sharing a successful teaching strategy with colleagues or conferring informally with a colleague who is concerned about connecting with a new student. In this chapter, I explore two aspects of collaborative work that teacher leaders can focus on to maximize their efforts toward peer support and student improvement: (1) classroom-level collaboration, such as mentoring new teachers and holding collaborative meetings, and (2) schoolwide collaborative planning and connection with families.

CLASSROOM COLLABORATION

When faced with questions, concerns, suggestions, and ideas, professionals of all types have a natural need to turn to someone they respect. For teachers, this need generates collaboration at the classroom level that receives little formal recognition but, arguably, is the most crucial factor in getting new teachers through the early years and in sustaining a strong sense of job satisfaction for experienced teachers. Writing for the National Education Association, longtime educator Sabrina Gates (2018) describes the impact informal collaboration with colleagues has had on her and on her students:

> Working with a small group of trusted teachers gave me the opportunity to turn what I thought was a silly idea at the time into a unique and creative lesson plan. . . . Peer-to-peer collaboration can turn a small idea into the seeds for something fabulous. . . . When we work together, we create a better learning experience. Teacher collaboration positively impacts student achievement, and allows us to explore new territory.

Gates's experience is confirmed by academic studies of the impact that collaboration has on teachers and their students. David Schleifer, Chloe Rinehart, and Tess Yanisch's (2017) meta-study on teacher collaboration, titled *Teacher Collaboration in Perspective: A Guide to Research*, validates this experience: "Research has shown that schools in which teacher collaboration is encouraged tend to have higher student achievement than less collaborative schools" (p. 9). The findings hold true "even when controlling for student demographics, school size, proportion of low-income and minority students and other factors" (Schleifer et al., 2017, p. 10). The meta-study also indicates that a collaborative environment is beneficial for student teachers as well as those who are already in-service.

Education researcher John Hattie developed a way of ranking influences—positive and negative—on educational outcomes, using what are called *effect sizes* to express the differences in efficacy among influences as numbers. Over time, he ranked 256 influences. Hattie uses 0.40, which is the average effect size, as a hinge point to identify what works well and what doesn't (Visible Learning, 2018). By far, the highest-ranked influence is collective teacher efficacy, which is the focus of this chapter. The other items in the top five, expressed along with their effect sizes in the following list, are closely related to research and professional learning (chapter 3, page 43) and renewal and improvement of instruction and student learning (chapter 4, page 61).

1. Collective teacher efficacy (1.57)

2. Self-reported grades (1.33)

3. Teacher estimates of achievement (1.29)

4. Cognitive task analysis (1.29)

5. Response to intervention (1.29)

A collaborative culture results in high levels of collective teacher efficacy and promotes strong connections among educators, families, and the school community as a whole.

Teacher collaboration has the advantage of being accessible to any teacher at any time. A teacher might initiate collaboration through something as simple as texting colleagues to ask if they know where the manual for the Cuisenaire rods is while the teacher is preparing a lesson that uses mathematics manipulatives. The focus can be specific and timely enough to deal with an emerging classroom-level need. This kind of spontaneous collaboration can last for a few hours or many months. It gives teachers a chance to get to know one another and develop the trust that makes sharing concerns and problems possible.

In a teacher leader's classroom, methods and materials are continually tested against the specific needs of the students actually in the room at any given time (see chapter 3, page 43). Teacher leaders are informed about emerging issues in education and are fearless about trying new methods and materials that may better meet student needs.

But teacher leaders need to reach beyond their own classrooms and collaborate with colleagues for the work that begins in the classroom to achieve its full potential in the grade level or content area and, ultimately, in the school as a whole. Professional learning community architect Richard DuFour dedicated his career to helping educators engage in productive collaboration, including being very clear about what collaboration must entail in order for it to influence classroom and school practices (DuFour, DuFour, Eaker, Many, & Mattos, 2016).

Despite compelling evidence that working collaboratively represents best practice (Azorín & Fullan, 2022; Surr et al., 2018), teachers in many schools continue to work in isolation. Even in schools that endorse the idea of collaboration, staff's willingness to collaborate often stops at the classroom door. Some schools equate the term *collaboration* with congeniality and focus on building group camaraderie. In other schools, staff members join forces to develop consensus on operational procedures, such as how they will respond to tardiness or supervise recess. Still others organize staff members into committees to oversee different facets of school operation, such as discipline, technology, and social climate. Although each of these activities can serve a useful purpose, none represents the kind of professional dialogue that can transform a school into a professional learning community (DuFour et al., 2016).

Engaging in meaningful, impactful professional dialogue isn't easy. Teachers are under a lot of pressure to be authority figures, so they find it hard to admit a mistake or pose a question that reveals a lack of knowledge. But this kind of honest conversation is key to building collective teacher efficacy, especially when teacher practices around essential learning goals are at stake.

How to teach reading is a case in point. Over time, two major factions have developed around how students learn to read: (1) whole language and (2) phonics, also known as the science of reading. The whole-language approach to teaching reading gained traction to such an extent that materials developed by Lucy Calkins (2000) and her team at Columbia University's Teachers College became widely used in schools across the United States. Calkins's (2000) book *The Art of Teaching Reading* is a foundational source for taking what she and her team describe as a "balanced literacy" approach. Calkins (2015, 2023) developed a reading curriculum called *Units of Study in Reading*, which is based on the idea that students are natural readers when they receive appealing materials to choose from and reading is not confined to structured tasks. As natural readers, students are encouraged to notice clues to meaning, such as illustrations, but not taught to sound out words using phonics. Education journalist and author Dana Goldstein (2022), writing for *The New York Times*, makes the point that "classroom practice has lurched back and forth, with phonics going in and out of style."

Advocates of the science of reading, citing the evidence of many years of brain research, point out:

> Functional magnetic resonance imaging of the brain demonstrates that humans process written language letter by letter, sound by sound. Far from

being automatic, reading requires a rewiring of the brain, which is primed by evolution to recognize faces, not words. (Goldstein, 2022)

Even Calkins has modified her approach to include phonics. She published a phonics supplement in 2018 and an updated version of *Units of Study in Reading* in 2023, but Goldstein (2022) notes that Calkins "still believes in peer collaboration during phonics lessons, and in silent reading for kindergartners who are primarily looking at pictures. Critics see those activities as a waste of precious classroom minutes."

When opinion about something as important as teaching reading is so divided, it can cause a rift in a school community. Such conflict can tempt teachers to retreat into the classroom and close the door. But in a collaborative school culture where teacher leaders make the effort to connect with colleagues and build trust, it will be possible to engage in honest conversations about fraught topics and keep classroom doors—and minds—open to time-tested strategies and hot-off-the-presses research. In my experience, no single method or set of materials works all the time for all students. Teacher leaders stay in touch with emerging research and respect long-standing strategies that show continued evidence of effectiveness. Teacher leaders listen and follow through on colleagues' suggestions as well as offer their own. In the case of reading instruction, a teacher leader would likely decide to experiment with integrating phonics instruction with whole-language practices in order to best meet student needs. But that would be just the beginning of collaboration on reading instruction because the teacher leader would invite a colleague in to observe these experiments and talk about how to improve them. And the teacher leader would visit other classrooms to see how ideas colleagues have shared are working out. The approach to reading instruction will continue to evolve; the constant is the support and encouragement teacher leaders offer colleagues in a collaborative culture.

Methods and materials change over time, but what teachers believe and convey with conviction to students tends to promote learning. What is important is that teachers are making informed, conscious decisions about what is good for students. Classroom collaboration gives teachers the opportunity to see colleagues in action and to grapple with the idea that effective teaching can't just be downloaded from a universal program. Keeping an open mind about what works makes it possible for teachers to learn from one another as well as from their own trial and error. Teachers continually fine-tune methods and materials to meet students' needs, increase engagement in learning, and contribute to students' confidence as well as academic success. A teacher leader goes a step further, doing the research, weighing the pros and cons of one approach or another, conducting experiments, studying results, and reaching out to colleagues to share results. Teacher leaders' contributions to a collaborative culture create a rich learning environment in which teachers at all levels of experience can develop insights and hone skills. Two facets of collaboration that teacher leaders can focus on are (1) creating a collegial safety net for new teachers and (2) organizing and encouraging others to organize grade-level and content-area collaborative meetings.

Collegial Safety Net

Teacher collaboration isn't just about finding new and effective ways to enhance student learning. It's also about having a sense of safety as a teacher, that feeling that you're not alone in the work you do. This is important for all teachers, but it's especially so for those who are new to teaching. Research shows that a collaborative climate is good for both teachers and students, and it's especially beneficial for new teachers (Schleifer et al., 2017). Whether they are just out of college or have turned to education after a career in another field, teachers new to the classroom need a safety net to get through the challenges of the first year or two. Some of those challenges are generated by the steep learning curve that comes with managing and teaching in a classroom. But some of them are due to external social and economic factors. Three of these challenges that tend to trip up new teachers—and can give even experienced teachers trouble—are (1) stress and burnout, (2) formal evaluations, and (3) teacher-student dynamics.

Stress and Burnout

In an article for *NEA Today*, writer and editor Tim Walker (2022) notes that "underlying factors have been corroding the stability of the profession at least since the economic crisis of 2009–10 and the staggering education budget cuts that emerged in its wake." These underlying factors are interrelated, and they intensified during the COVID-19 pandemic: increased responsibilities to cover staff shortages, low pay, assignments for which teachers are unprepared, and insufficient time to get to know students. Teacher leaders can especially help mitigate these factors because of their dual role; a teacher leader experiences school as a teacher and as a leader, aware of both internal and external challenges. A teacher new to the classroom may try to make things look as if everything is OK, but a teacher leader who is sensitive to the stress new teachers experience can help a new colleague articulate and manage feelings of frustration and fear of failure. Putting such feelings in words makes it possible for a teacher leader to respond, "I know how that feels," and "The first year is hard, but it will get better." As education and leadership expert Douglas Reeves (2021) points out, "Individual heroism is not a sustainable strategy for schools" (p. 88). A teacher new to the profession needs to know there is a collegial safety net in place.

Whether teachers are new to teaching or seasoned veterans, their work in and out of the classroom doesn't always go as planned. We educators make mistakes. Unexpected problems arise. Questions accumulate. Teachers should never feel alone as they seek improvement, overcome challenges, and answer difficult questions. New teachers need time to develop a kind of sixth sense about students, which helps teachers decide what strategies will work with the students who are actually in the room on any given day. Not knowing how students will respond to a given strategy or activity is exhausting and demoralizing. Further, students experience change over time, and how they respond to the same teaching strategies isn't static. This is the learning curve that even veteran teachers must negotiate in order to continue in the profession. The curve is steep. Without a supportive school culture, research shows:

> Nearly half of new teachers leave the classroom in their first five years, including 9.5 percent in the first year alone. Nearly a third of those leaving their positions [choose] to leave the profession altogether, opting for careers outside of education. (Abitabile, 2020)

Within a school culture where collaboration is common and its value for both teachers and students is recognized, the likelihood that a new teacher will receive the support necessary to thrive increases.

Schleifer and colleagues (2017) draw from a thorough article published in the *Educational Research Review* that presents a meta-review of eighty-two studies and looks closely at how collaboration influences teachers (Vangrieken, Dochy, Raes, & Kyndt, 2015). The review is candid, acknowledging that it can be difficult to untangle how collaboration specifically factors into an array of steps a school or district can take to create a positive environment. Possible benefits of teacher collaboration are listed with qualifiers:

- Schools with lower teacher turnover tend to be more collaborative.
- There is some limited evidence of a relationship between teacher job satisfaction, teacher collaboration, and student achievement.
- Collaboration among teachers may do more to advance teachers' instructional practices than do learning opportunities for individual teachers.
- Teachers have been found to value collaboration for a variety of reasons, including moral support, but sometimes voice concerns and report experiencing conflict.

- Collaboration involves vulnerability and difficult discussions among teachers. (Schleifer et al., 2017, p. 15)

Yet the review concludes that "collaboration is associated with teachers progressing in their job performance and on a personal level in terms of feeling more motivated, experiencing less isolation and having better morale" (Vangrieken et al., 2015). The review also makes it clear that researchers have seen a significant connection between teacher collaboration and student achievement (Vangrieken et al., 2015). A teacher leader can share hard-earned experience with the learning curve and encourage colleagues of any experience level to look back from time to time and celebrate how much ground they have already covered. For a teacher facing burnout, this valuable perspective can be life changing.

As educators, no matter our level of experience, we are all on a continuum of teaching, somewhere between the worst lesson we have taught and the perfect lesson we aspire to teach. We move forward and backward on this continuum as we gain more experience and our expectations of ourselves become more complex. And we all need support, encouragement, follow-up, and honest feedback. A teacher leader can help in three crucial ways.

1. **Get to know colleagues, especially new teachers, well enough to understand their strengths and needs:** Have honest conversations about both so the colleagues can build confidence based on strengths and be open to help in areas of need. When there is much to do and time is short, it's tempting to focus on what needs work rather than on what works well. But it's a real confidence builder for a teacher leader to say something like, "Your students really enjoy writing in their journals to start the class," or "Your students say what they think during discussions, which tells me you've earned their trust."

2. **Participate in or propose collaborations that pair teachers whose strengths and needs are complementary:** Teachers whose profiles are similar are likely to have already found each other. Helping teachers form alliances with colleagues whose profiles are different can benefit both. It could be that an experienced teacher is struggling with technology that is second nature to a new teacher while the new teacher is struggling with the timing of activities in the classroom, which is second nature to the experienced teacher.

3. **Encourage teachers to focus on making school a positive experience for students:** Substantial research agrees on an important point—student engagement is a key factor in academic success (Olson & Peterson, 2015, citing Fredricks, Blumenfeld, & Paris, 2004; Skinner, Furrer, Marchand, & Kindermann, 2008).

    Teachers can show students they are known and respected by taking the time to establish a positive relationship with each one. This gives the students a sense of belonging and creates the conditions in which students can engage with learning in the classroom and in school as a whole. More detailed suggestions are included in the chart of teacher leader actions (figure 1.1, page 10). Briefly, teachers can show respect for students in the following ways.

    ✦ Provide individualized feedback, and ask students for feedback (and use it).

    ✦ Help students connect with other students through collaborative work.

    ✦ Invite students' lives into the classroom, and share your life with the students.

    ✦ Provide challenging assignments, and make it OK to fail and try again.

    ✦ Maintain high standards, but emphasize learning over grades.

    ✦ Include students in the assessment process.

    ✦ Balance teaching time with time for rest and recreation.

New teachers who receive opportunities to get to know and collaborate with other teachers and who understand that students must feel known and respected in order to be ready to learn are well on the way to developing effective teaching practices that will help students experience success, build confidence, and find joy in learning, as well as reduce their own stress and burnout.

When you identify a teacher who is struggling, you can make yourself available for some informal collaboration on lesson plans. Informal opportunities to walk colleagues through a lesson plan help them notice potential problems. In turn, having the opportunity to listen to other teachers' plans broadens the range of what is possible for you and other colleagues. For example, there are many ways to organize lesson plans. New teachers, especially early in that first year, may be tempted to script every word they plan to say and every response they hope to receive from students. There are two problems with trying to stick to a script: (1) it makes it easy to get lost in the details and lose sight of the lesson's larger purpose, and (2) it makes it hard to take advantage of emergent teachable moments. Go back in time with me to the first meeting with my first American literature class. I had spent not just hours but days and weeks developing lesson plans for the course. Because I was new, it hadn't hit me that trying to keep my place in the elaborate lesson plan would prevent me from really seeing the students in the room, who were hoping the new teacher would make sense and the class would be worthwhile. It took me a few days to realize that all my hard work on the content would be wasted if I couldn't engage with the students. Once I got my priorities in order, I was able to shift the focus from asking, "What is American literature?" to asking, "Why does American literature matter to me and to you?" That shift in focus made working together to form collaborative groups around half a dozen novels and getting to know one another possible.

While providing words of commiseration and validating the problems teachers are facing are both powerful ways to help, teacher leaders are also uniquely positioned to offer teachers concrete ideas that might help root out the causes of stress and burnout. Teacher leaders can share approaches to planning that have worked for them or other colleagues and encourage new teachers to plan lessons around well-established concepts like learning goals and essential questions. An organizational tool such as the lesson-planning chart in figure 2.1 can help. This example maps key aspects of a lesson sequence designed for fifth graders. It integrates elements of geography, science, and social studies. A reproducible version suitable for any lesson or grade level is available on page 39.

You can keep a copy of the learning goals your students are expected to achieve close at hand and encourage other teachers to do the same. Making it a personal rule to identify specific learning goals for each lesson and to share those goals with students means teachers will always be ready for classroom visits and any questions an observer might have about the purpose of the lesson. Not only will the teacher be able to respond to such questions, but students will be able to do so as well.

Formal Evaluations

A teacher leader can also help colleagues prepare for formal evaluations that states or provinces typically require. When I first started teaching, formal evaluations were infrequent and perfunctory. But the National Council on Teacher Quality's (2019) *State of the States* report on teacher and principal evaluation policy points out that

Learning goals: Use literacy, inquiry, and collaboration to better understand the relationship between human culture and the natural world.

Essential question: What does it take to make a home?

Key features	Gender expectations	Cultural norms	Habits of school	Special considerations
Primary resources Books read out loud *Need a House? Call Ms. Mouse!* by George Mendoza *Wonderful Houses Around the World* by Yoshio Komatsu	The protagonist of *Need a House?* is a female architect.	Instead of boxy houses, Ms. Mouse designs homes that fit her clients' lives.	The focus is on generating imaginative answers to the essential question rather than finding the right answer.	The books are accessible and the images will help students develop a broad interpretation of "home."
Supplemental materials Film *Animal Homes: Cities,* PBS Nature		The film is rated PG for evolutionary approach and some content that might raise issues, depending on community norms.		There are three episodes. Episode 1 is sufficient. Preview it to confirm compatibility with community values.
Independent reading suggestions from Liz Lesnick (n.d.) for Read Brightly: • *Home* by Carson Ellis • *A House Is a House for Me* by Mary Ann Hoberman, illustrated by Betty Fraser • *The House That's Your Home* by Sally Lloyd-Jones, illustrated by Jane Dyer • *My House / Mi Casa* by Rebecca Emberley • *This Is Our House* by Hyewon Yum • *Two Homes* by Claire Masurel, illustrated by Kady MacDonald Denton • *Welcome Home, Bear: A Book of Animal Habitats* by Il Sung Na				Students who are or have been unhoused may welcome the opportunity to read and talk about home but need extra support to deal with this topic.
Formative activities Initial response to essential question Listening and viewing journal with both written and sketched notes and reflection			Provide comments, suggestions, and encouragement, but no grades.	Provide opportunities for students to share excerpts with the class.
Performance tasks Solo or paired: Visual representation of home (drawing, model, collage, and so on) Small group: Performance of multivoiced poem that weaves together images, experiences, and ideas about home from all members of the group				Invite family to view projects and hear multivoiced poems.

FIGURE 2.1: Sample lesson-planning chart.

most U.S. states are changing evaluation policy so that evaluation is useful to new teachers and fair to all teachers.

Implicit in formal classroom observation is acknowledgment that teaching is both art and science. The science might be measured through formative and summative assessment results, but the art requires experienced observation. A collaborative climate helps all teachers by providing opportunities to observe colleagues (formally or informally) and receive feedback. A teacher leader can help colleagues understand what an observer conducting a formal observation might be looking for in areas such as the following.

- There is evidence of rapport and respect between teacher and students.
- There is evidence of rapport and respect among students.
- Work students are asked to do aligns with district and state or provincial learning goals.
- Students understand the purpose of their work.
- The teacher provides guidelines to help students experience success.
- Students work in multiple configurations: whole class, groups, and pairs.
- Students turn to both teacher and peers for feedback.

Sometimes teachers who are worried about losing control of the classroom may spend too much time on small student behaviors, putting names on the board, imposing penalties, and so on. This is often the case for new teachers. Further, students may test a new teacher, so it takes some conscious restraint to let small things go and save class time and penalties for behaviors that cross the line. Alternatively, some teachers get along with students by asking little and overlooking too much. Teacher leaders who get to know their colleagues can head off problems early, before they jeopardize both teacher effectiveness and student success. New teachers especially benefit from finding a balance between overreaction and firm but fair follow-through when needed. Teacher leaders know that students who feel known and respected are likely to return that respect to their teacher, making classroom management not a contest but an additional form of collaboration—one between students and teacher (Terada, 2021).

Youki Terada (2021) tracks research trends for Edutopia and helps ensure that each writing is engaging, relevant, and backed by research. His article "How Novice and Expert Teachers Approach Classroom Management Differently" is characteristically well substantiated and makes the concept of "invisible" classroom management accessible. He cites that while novice teachers rely on routines and consequences, essentially following a script when it comes to managing students' behavior, expert teachers have "adaptive expertise" that allows them to draw from various strategies depending on the context (Stahnke & Blömeke, 2021).

Terada (2021) offers half a dozen specific strategies, all of them designed to build relationships and increase engagement with content. (See also figure 1.1, page 10, for a summary of actions typical of teacher leaders, which contribute to collaborative relationships between teacher and students.)

With support from teacher leaders, formal evaluation can be a positive process that builds trust and contributes to each teacher's confidence. To have value for teachers, formal evaluation should include conversations before and after classroom visits. This sequence gives teachers the opportunity to share and discuss their plans with observers, creating a window for modification, if needed. It also gives teachers a chance to reflect on how the observed classes went, which can be a useful indicator of teachers' strengths and areas for development as educators.

Teacher-Student Dynamics

How an experienced teacher interacts with students is partly a matter of personality and partly a deliberate balance between encouragement and expectation. In the case of new high school teachers, who may not be much older than the juniors and seniors they teach, it can be difficult to transition from being a student to being the adult in the room. New elementary teachers may find it just as hard to find the right response to younger students who love their teacher unconditionally and want to show their love with hugs and snuggles. It's important to get to know students and to nurture positive relationships with them, but personal warmth needs to be balanced with professional responsibility.

What preservice teachers learn about the ethical obligations of educators may seem irrelevant in the heady atmosphere of a classroom full of students who think their teacher is cool. A teacher leader can keep an eye on how things are going and, if necessary, help a colleague understand the difference between positive relationships with students and relationships that are inappropriate. The website of the National Association of State Directors of Teacher Education and Certification (NASDTEC, 2021) provides a code of ethics that includes responsibility to students; this means, in short, how teachers treat their students. According to NASDTEC (2021), teachers should respect students' dignity, safety, and well-being by modeling healthy boundaries—that is, being cognizant of their mode and tone of communication, the appropriateness of settings in which they interact, and the possible impact of their cultural backgrounds and identities. NASDTEC (2021) also stresses the importance of propriety in matters of dress, physical contact, gift giving or receiving, and relationships. New teachers may need help in knowing exactly where these boundaries must be; teacher leaders can gently provide it.

It can be devastating to a new teacher when enthusiasm for students is interpreted as inappropriate. A perception of this nature, even when it's mistaken, can do lasting damage to a teacher's credibility. Talking about such matters isn't easy. Initiating a conversation about professional propriety takes courage and kindness. But courage and kindness are qualities that teacher leaders possess in abundance. Teacher leaders can help those new to the profession find a good balance between human warmth and professional responsibility.

Collaborative Meetings

Meetings are endemic in a school community. I like the *Cambridge Dictionary* definition of *meeting*, which is "a planned occasion when people come together, either in person or online (= using the internet), to discuss something" (Meeting, n.d.). Meetings can be tense, intensely boring, or even inspiring, and they are also always necessary. The format of meetings at the district and building levels may be constrained by the need to follow a specific process. But smaller recurring meetings, such as weekly or monthly grade-level or content-area meetings, can be organized collaboratively; this gives teachers responsibility for generating and prioritizing topics and deciding what approach will work best with each one. Possible approaches may include whole-group discussion, small-group conversations followed by shared findings, presentations by teams of teachers with a shared interest, joint meetings with another grade level or content area, and so on. Although there are limits to what can be achieved in an hour, there is no limit to the relevance and value that recurring meetings can achieve when developed collaboratively, and those hours can add up to shared knowledge and increased respect for colleagues.

Team members can design collaborative meetings around a set of predictable features that promote quality of information, interaction among participants, relevance of content and materials, active engagement with content and materials, and follow-up. The elements of an effective collaborative meeting include the following.

- **Discussion and presentation:** As members of a grade level or content area take turns leading discussion and presenting information, they have great opportunities to practice teaching strategies that seem to work with students on their adult colleagues. The goals certainly are the same in the sense of trying to get everyone involved in speaking and active listening and providing useful information in an accessible, relevant, and memorable way. Visuals can help, but don't depend on them too much. The most meaningful collaborative meetings get their energy from honest, energetic discussion.

- **Background information:** Important topics in education are complicated. The information you provide needs to be backed up with reliable sources. You might end up with a thick packet of background information as you prepare for presentation, but you must resist the temptation to make a copy for everyone. Ahead of time, send everyone a short article that is intriguing and can be read quickly. At the meeting, provide a list of major points with room for notes and a list of resources for follow-up. You can, of course, offer more information to anyone who wants a deeper dive.

- **Collaboration:** Just as students in your classroom need alternation among presentation of information, small-group discussion, and individual reflection, your colleagues need the same kind of alternation at collaborative meetings. What your colleagues take away from a meeting may include a meaningful conversation with the person next to them or a reflective note to self.

- **Application:** Again, just as students need some way to experiment with what you're teaching them, colleagues need an opportunity to at least think about how they might apply what you present to improve instruction and student learning. You could ask colleagues to each write one thing they might do on an index card, which you could then collect and transcribe as follow-up.

- **Follow-up:** Some colleagues may accept your offer of more information, so that's one form of follow-up already built into the meeting. Sharing colleagues' ideas about applying the information is another kind of follow-up. In addition, you could ask colleagues to complete a chart like the one in figure 2.2 (page 30) that includes an invitation to request further study. The chart is formatted so teacher leaders can use it to have attendees reflect privately or to gather attendee feedback.

Elements of a collaborative meeting	Comments
Discussion and presentation: What did you learn from the discussion or presentation about the topic (or about discussion or presentation strategies)?	
Background information: What impact did the background information sent before the meeting have on what you learned from today's meeting?	
Collaboration: What stood out for you most today about your colleagues' responses to the topic?	
Application: How will you use what you learned about today's topic to improve instruction and student learning?	
Follow-up: What follow-up would you like to see on this topic?	

FIGURE 2.2: Interactive chart of elements of a collaborative meeting.

*Visit **go.SolutionTree.com/teacherefficacy** for a free reproducible version of this figure.*

Through encouragement of informal classroom collaboration, maintenance of a collegial safety net, and support of collaborative meetings, teacher leaders contribute to a collaborative climate that makes it possible for colleagues to feel known and respected. A collaborative climate allows teachers—both new and experienced—to cultivate a sense of belonging and freedom to engage deeply, try new things, and experience success.

A CONNECTED SCHOOL COMMUNITY

Teacher leaders, when acting as conduits between classroom and office, fulfill a unique and essential role within the school. The focus of this book is teacher leadership and, in part, how that differs from school leadership. Teacher leaders, as explained in the introduction, are not administrators, but collaboration between teacher leaders (with their strong connections at the classroom level) and administrators (with their responsibilities at the school and district levels) can have a tremendously positive impact on schoolwide culture. School leaders who respect and support the important role teacher leaders play and are willing to share authority with them can generate the respect that keeps lines of communication open between the classroom and the school office. This sense of connectedness especially has a bearing on schoolwide planning and connections with families.

Schoolwide Planning

School planning might be more efficient as a top-down process, but the results will work better for students if the process includes collaboration with teachers. For example, teaching schedules can be efficiently developed by plugging the relevant information into a computer program, but the schedules will be greatly improved if teacher leaders have the opportunity to gather information from colleagues about their needs and wishes and provide this information to the scheduling team. This might involve teacher leaders' meeting with the team to discuss teacher preferences or actually drafting a possible schedule focused on teacher preferences. Theoretically, teachers should be able to carry out any assignments in the grade levels and content areas for which they have earned certification. In practice, teachers have strengths, weaknesses, interests, and affinities that need to be taken into consideration. In addition, teaching assignments need to evolve over time, again finding a balance between what the teacher already does well and what will allow for some exploration and growth. This might mean a change in grade level or the addition of a new course.

In order to gather these data, teacher leaders can survey colleagues about teaching preferences, using tools such as figure 2.3.

Please list in order of preference the three grade levels or courses you would most like to teach. Comment on what you like about each one.

Grade or course 1: _____

Comment: _____

Grade or course 2: _____

Comment: _____

Grade or course 3: _____

Comment: _____

Please mention any additional role you would be interested in playing to meet student needs, support colleagues, and interact with the community.

FIGURE 2.3: Survey of course preferences.

*Visit **go.SolutionTree.com/teacherefficacy** for a free reproducible version of this figure.*

Primary classroom teachers work with a single group of students on a broad range of subjects. Secondary classroom teachers and specialists at both levels work with multiple groups of students on a single subject area, from art to zoology. Although secondary classroom teachers focus on a single subject area, it's typical for them to be assigned multiple *preps*, meaning they would need to prepare lessons for several different courses or academic levels. When I surveyed high school English department members about limiting their preps to two, they weren't interested. The details varied, but the consistent theme was their desire for variety and balance. One member especially enjoyed working with ninth graders, but she liked to work with all three academic levels the school offered (college prep A, college prep B, and honors). Another member found the contrast between ninth graders and twelfth graders stimulating. A third believed it was important for him to have thorough knowledge of required courses, but he also enjoyed teaching senior electives. I find this desire for variety and balance applies across grade levels and content areas. Last year's teaching assignment may not meet this year's needs and wishes. It's important to ask and keep asking what will work best each year. It's also important to keep lines of communication between the classroom and the school office open and active.

In addition to their contributions to the all-important teaching schedule, teacher leaders can gather information about preferences related to the room or rooms in which colleagues teach. The details of such a survey will vary tremendously based on the school context, from a primary school to a secondary one and from a small rural school to a large urban one. But the importance of gathering information remains consistent across the board. Figure 2.4 provides a sample of how such a survey might be set up.

Please rate the following factors according to their importance to you and your students.

1 = Very important

2 = Somewhat important

3 = Not important

_____ Natural light

_____ Location near the school office

_____ Location near the school library

_____ Student desk units

_____ Student tables and chairs

_____ Teacher desk

_____ Teacher laptop stand

_____ Counter space

_____ Secure storage space

_____ Other

Please describe the technology support you need in the classroom:

FIGURE 2.4: Sample room-preference survey.

*Visit **go.SolutionTree.com/teacherefficacy** for a free reproducible version of this figure.*

Preference surveys and time for collaboration between teachers and teacher leaders and between teacher leaders and members of the scheduling team contribute to construction of a schedule that grants as many wishes and meets as many needs as possible. The time taken to share information and the desire to create the best possible schedule for everyone achieve results beyond what a computer can generate. A schedule that works well is an affirmation of what people can achieve in a collaborative, connected school culture. Schoolwide planning allows everyone to face the challenges of a new year of teaching and learning knowing their needs and wishes have been heard and respected.

Connections With Families

Because family involvement in school makes a significant difference in the quality of a student's educational experience, connecting with families is one of the most important domains of teacher leadership.

According to a Global Family Research Project (2018a) report commissioned by the Carnegie Corporation of New York, over fifty years of research confirms that family involvement in school has a powerful impact on "children's development, educational attainment, and success in school and life" (p. 3). This report builds on a solid foundation of studies by researchers such as Karen Bogenschneider and Carol Johnson (2004), who remind us that schools may have changed over time, but families still play a central role in the academic success of their children: "Families continue to retain primary authority and responsibility for their children's education in legal order, moral authority, and social thought" (p. 5).

Bogenschneider and Johnson's (2004) report makes the point that research consistently finds families remain the primary "influence on their children's development and school success" (p. 2), as shown by five measures of success.

1. Students whose families are involved in school earn higher grades and test scores.

2. Attendance records show that students with family support have low absence rates.

3. Dropout rates for students whose families express interest in school are low.

4. When families participate in students' education, the students have ambitious aspirations.

5. Students exhibit more positive attitudes toward school and homework when they know their families care about their success.

The research also indicates that "parental school involvement seems most important for those children who need it most—children growing up in disadvantaged, highly-stressed families" (Bogenschneider & Johnson, 2004, p. 2). The authors cite Harvard professor Robert Putnam's assertion that "given a choice between a 10% increase in school budgets or a 10% increase in parent involvement, he would invest in parent involvement" (Bogenschneider & Johnson, 2004, p. 1).

Follow-up research suggests that the positive impact of family involvement holds regardless of which parent is involved, how much or how little education the parent has received, ethnicity, or family configuration. A meta-analysis of families' impact on school, based on the synthesis of 448 independent studies, shows small but consistent positive associations between parental involvement and academic achievement, engagement, and motivation as well as social and emotional adjustment (Barger, Kim, Kuncel, & Pomerantz, 2019). Similar to previous studies, "there was little variation due to age, ethnicity, or socioeconomic status in the links between different types of involvement and children's academic adjustment" (Barger et al., 2019). However, it's important to note that parental involvement has an overall positive impact on engagement and motivation, but the impact shifts to negative for academic achievement when parents assist with homework. Collaboration works wonders, but there are times when independent work is essential because of the growth that can occur when students are allowed to take risks, fail, try again, and, at last, succeed on their own and in their own way.

The Global Family Research Project (2018a) shows that when families and schools connect in five specific areas, they are more effective at improving learning and promoting student success.

1. **Attendance:** When families set expectations for their children to attend school and make sure these expectations are met, they help prevent absenteeism.

2. **Data sharing:** Accessible, understandable, and actionable data help schools and families establish a firm foundation for student learning.

3. **Academic and social development:** Schools can champion family engagement strategies that help students develop in content areas like literacy and science. Since learning isn't limited to the classroom, families have a lot of power to influence their children's learning.

4. **Digital media:** Responsible use of digital media and devices provides ways for students and their families to learn and connect with ease.

5. **Transitions:** Schools can focus their family engagement strategies on underserved students to keep them engaged as they enter kindergarten, middle school, and high school, as well as other important transition points.

The Global Family Research Project (2018a) also highlights dramatic shifts in focus that have taken place since 2000. In the past, involving families may have felt a little less effortful than it currently does. When I first started teaching at Newtown High School in the early 1990s, it was not unusual to see a parent delivering a forgotten lunch in the cafeteria or popping into a classroom to hand off some car keys. But a horrifying series of school shootings changed everything (Cox et al., 2022; Reeping, Gobaud, Branas, & Rajan, 2021). If my fellow teachers and I saw an adult in the hall without a visitor's pass thereafter, we asked, "May I help you?" and waited for an answer. Over time, I've seen doors locked, surveillance cameras installed, movement into and within the building monitored, and visitors required to check in and obtain passes. No school can relax its safety procedures. We educators need the plans and the drills. But we also need strong connections with family members and family involvement in school.

My work with two colleagues on a book for families called *High Stakes High School* (Zmuda, Tomaino, & Miller, 2001) included focus groups that revealed families may be intimidated by the bureaucracy of the school, and they may fear that drawing attention to their child will backfire. In my experience, families have other obstacles to overcome as well, including dealing with language barriers and simply finding time to meet with a teacher when they are working two jobs or have other children in other schools who also need support. The Global Family Research Project (2018b) urges educators to understand the diverse circumstances families may be dealing with while, at the same time, doing what it takes to connect with families:

> Not only do educators and policymakers need to understand the context in which families live, they also need to employ empathy based on the knowledge of what families desire and value. To do this, we must change the narrative to interrupt negative perceptions of low-income parents and parents of color [and] build public understanding of parents' essential role in achieving positive outcomes for their children.

People—whether family members or teachers—are not at their best when they are feeling inadequate and anxious. A teacher leader will look at such a situation from two perspectives: (1) teachers need support, and (2) families need encouragement to connect with school. Once it's clear to family members that the teacher's goal is not to be right but to find a way forward that is good for the student, a meeting can move from defense to collaboration.

It's important to keep in mind that families may have more than one school-age child. Let's say a family has three children in three different classes in elementary school or, perhaps, one child in each of three different schools—elementary, middle, and high school—or three children in high school taking a wide array of courses in different subjects and levels. In such cases, the information sent home has the potential to be overwhelming. The tone, clarity, and inclusiveness of classroom handouts, newsletters, and webpages can play large roles in how genuinely welcome families feel as partners in education. You, as a teacher leader, can help by encouraging colleagues in the same grade level or content area to collaborate on how they communicate shared expectations to families. It could sometimes be helpful to look through, for example, back-to-school handouts from teachers in the same grade level or content area and chart what topics the handouts include. A sample of such a chart is provided in figure 2.5.

Topic	Teacher A	Teacher B	Teacher C	Teacher D
Contact information	x	x	x	x
School mission				x
Learning goals	x	x	x	x
Essential questions		x	x	x
Texts and materials	x	x	x	x
Projects and activities	x	x		x
Performance tasks	x	x	x	x
Opportunities to volunteer	x	x		x

FIGURE 2.5: Sample chart of topics included in back-to-school handouts.

A chart such as the one in figure 2.5 encourages teachers to aim for greater consistency while respecting each teacher's individual approach. The goal is that everything developed for and shared with families do not just distribute information but communicate respectfully with a diverse audience.

In his article about partnering with parents, instructional supervisor Amir Taron Ayres (2022) candidly discusses ways that educators sometimes fall into *us* and *them* when thinking about families, focusing on communication barriers rather than ways around them and on what families might not be able to do rather than on what they can do and are doing:

> Every parent is different. The parents and guardians of our students are small business owners, nine-to-fivers, gig workers who manage multiple jobs, and stay-at-home caregivers. Establishing strong partnerships with parents through effective communication involves a willingness to be flexible with our mode of messaging. For those of us who are introverts, this does mean that we will have to pick up the phone sometimes.

Some family members may appreciate a phone call and the human voice on the other end of the line. Some may prefer an email or text they can respond to at a convenient moment. As a teacher leader, just as you understand the importance of getting to know students, you must get to know families. You can ask for preferences at back-to-school night and also send a survey home so each family has multiple opportunities to let you know what method of contact they prefer, when is a good time, and what language is preferred. In turn, you can make it easy for families to get in touch by offering a variety of contact options. If problems do come up, already being in cordial contact with families will make finding solutions easier.

A common strategy for making positive contact with families is to contact them when there is good news to report. Ayres (2022) sends positive text messages about "student effort, improved behavior, and class participation during class" and "would even send an occasional picture of an engaged student." The messages to family can also positively impact the students; Ayres (2022) recalls a student who was so used to negative messages that she didn't believe her teacher had actually seen her doing something constructive in class. He had to show her the photo to prove he had caught her being a good student. But Ayres (2022) cautions against trying to force a positive just to check a family off the list of weekly calls:

> Positive communication should not be disingenuous. Many teachers use the "compliment sandwich" when communicating with parents, saying something nice about a student in order to slip in the real issue, followed by more praise. While this is well-intentioned, parents do not take it as positive communication. What really matters to parents and guardians is whether or not we can express that we see and understand their children.

Teacher leaders take the time to get to know students because feeling known and having a sense of belonging positively impact student learning (Olson & Peterson, 2015, citing Fredricks et al., 2004; Skinner et al., 2008). And, equally important, knowledge of students that goes beyond grades and test scores is essential to effective communication and strong connections with families.

Building positive relationships with families will, in turn, contribute to the quality and capacity of individual classrooms and to the school community as a whole.

SUMMARY

This chapter explored collaboration at the classroom and school levels while also examining approaches to family communication that are respectful and effective. We also took a close look at the positive impact on learning that family involvement generates. The chapter included an opportunity to reflect on the content of communication with parents and consistency within grade levels and content areas. The chapter concludes on page 40 with small, doable steps teachers can take toward an increasingly collaborative and connected school culture. Chapter 3 continues the exploration of how to influence, support, and renew school communities with a focus on research and professional learning designed to meet student needs.

LESSON-PLANNING CHART

Learning goals:

Essential question:

Key features	Gender expectations	Cultural norms	Habits of school	Special considerations
Primary resources				
Supplemental materials				
Formative activities				
Performance tasks				

Teacher Leaders, Classroom Champions © 2023 Solution Tree Press ▪ SolutionTree.com
Visit **go.SolutionTree.com/teacherefficacy** to download this free reproducible.

NEXT STEPS FOR A COLLABORATIVE AND CONNECTED CULTURE

The following tool details some steps you can take to experiment with strategies for creating a collaborative and connected culture. For each step, note the date you tried it and reflect on how it went. *What did you do? How did it go? What would you change? What's next?* There are spaces available at the end for you to plan additional steps you can take toward teacher leadership.

Next Steps Tried	Date Tried	Reflection
Think about the context in which you teach and what opportunities and challenges are presented by this context.		
Identify a challenge that you and a colleague have in common, and decide on one step you will take together to address it.		
Identify what process your school uses to make teaching assignments. Determine whether it is working well, and locate one thing you could do to make it work better.		
Keeping in mind Amir Taron Ayres's (2022) comment, "What really matters to parents and guardians is whether or not we can express that we see and understand their children," challenge yourself to write a brief but specific description of each of your students.		

page 1 of 2

Collaborate with colleagues to increase the consistency of expectations that you share with families.				

Reference

Ayres, A. T. (2022, May 17). 3 tips for partnering with parents for student success. Accessed at www.edutopia.org/article/3-tips-partnering-parents-student-success on June 7, 2022.

CHAPTER 3

Research and Professional Learning to Meet Student Needs

As described in chapters 1 and 2, there are many ways that teacher leaders can exert a positive influence on the school community. The solid foundation on which a collaborative and connected school community is built is knowledge—knowledge of subject matter and educational approaches, of course, but also knowledge of what people (students, colleagues, and families) need in order to experience success. The focus of this chapter is the value of research and professional learning generated in the classroom. No off-the-shelf strategy or program can offer the same level of inherent validity and relevance that teacher leaders achieve through action research.

Action research begins with a question to answer or a problem to study. A good place to start is asking students what they need. When I asked my students, "What is one thing you would like to change about English class?" one student after another wanted fewer analytical essays and more creative writing. I embarked on a search for ways to integrate what seemed to be very different approaches to writing. This took me back to my notes from conferences and workshops and then forward to current articles in education journals. I found out that my students weren't the only ones who wanted more creativity mixed in with analysis. I began planning creative approaches to analytical writing, which eventually developed four key features: (1) students selected their own topics, (2) field research was combined with academic research, (3) creative writing added nuance to analytical writing, and (4) students were invited to reflect on the process.

As I talked with students about their works in progress, observed peer response sessions, and read the final drafts, it became clear that students had made progress in several pragmatic areas: fewer errors of usage, no issues with plagiarism, and no questions about how long the pieces needed to be. Even more important, students had worked hard and enjoyed the work. The unique topics, independent thinking, and various combinations of creative and analytical writing made the finished products both substantial and engaging. I enjoyed reading the work and, as they made clear in their reflections, students were proud to share their work with each other.

Activation of research in the classroom creates a dynamic cycle of information gathering, planning, and evaluation that continually improves instruction and student learning because teachers learn from each evaluation and use that learning to inform the next round. This dynamic cycle goes unremarked about every day in schools everywhere, but it's worth taking a close look at how classroom research works and why this research is so important. The topics relevant to classroom research are infinitely varied and are dependent on grade level, content area, student needs, and teacher perspective on teaching and learning. Teachers conduct research about methods, materials, content, learning goals, assessment, collaboration, self-direction, reflection—the list goes on and on. For demonstration purposes, this chapter focuses primarily on action research about formative rubric creation and self-assessment, but you can adapt the thinking and methods in this chapter to any topic. I discuss action research at the classroom level and the possibilities this research generates for professional learning at the school and district levels. I also explain how demonstration lessons can further teachers' professional learning.

CLASSROOM ACTION RESEARCH

Action research is intrinsically local—a single teacher focused on a classroom, a collaborative team focused on a course or grade level, a school trying to solve a problem. At each level, teacher leaders collect information and plan ways to renew instruction and improve student learning. Collaboration that goes beyond collegiality to test ideas and try new methods and materials entails risks: you have to admit what you don't yet know, a new approach might fail, and colleagues might disagree over what methods work best. But taking those risks builds trust, and trust is essential to a collaborative and connected school culture, as discussed in chapter 2 (page 15).

Teachers' working together creates "conditions for perpetual learning—an environment in which innovation and experimentation are viewed not as tasks to be accomplished or projects to be completed but as ways of conducting day-to-day business, *forever*" (DuFour et al., 2016, p. 13). Participation in classroom action research is accessible to every teacher, and the process can be both challenging and rewarding.

At the classroom level, action research might seem invisible, in the same way that classroom management is invisible when a teacher has earned students' respect. But in both cases, teacher leaders have goals based on student needs and engage in deliberate actions that meet those needs. It takes time and effort to get to know students and earn their respect. And it takes time and effort to identify an aspect of teaching and learning that could use improvement and then do something about it. The process of action research is multifaceted. *The Glossary of Education Reform* (2015) lists eight steps:

1. Identify a problem to be studied.
2. Collect data on the problem.
3. Organize, analyze, and interpret the data.
4. Develop a plan to address the problem.
5. Implement the plan.
6. Evaluate the results of the actions taken.
7. Identify a new problem.
8. Repeat the process.

The goal of action research is to address questions and problems that are practical and local and, in that process, also "make meaningful contributions to the larger body of knowledge and understanding in the field of education" (Glossary of Education Reform, 2015).

In the following sections, I highlight three areas of this process: (1) collect information and develop a plan, (2) implement the plan and evaluate the results, and (3) repeat the process.

Collect Information and Develop a Plan

Teacher leaders have infinite information available to them in print and online. The problem, of course, is figuring out what's worth time and effort. For books, I would go straight to Solution Tree's website (www.solutiontree.com) and browse the highly searchable catalog for the topics you're interested in developing in your classroom. Your school may have a grade-level or department budget for purchasing books. The school librarian may be interested in adding to a section containing professional publications. The principal may have discretionary funds that could be used to purchase books or subscriptions. The district may offer grants for materials that will contribute to professional learning and renewal of instruction. Asking for this kind of support can have the extra benefit of letting colleagues know about your interests so they can keep you in mind as other opportunities arise.

For information about and insight into what teachers across grades K–12 and content areas are currently doing that might help with my own research, I often turn to the carefully researched articles published by Edutopia (www.edutopia.org). These articles tend to feature links to background information, including research studies. Something that makes research exciting is the way one thing leads to another: one search term leads to a more specific one, a general-interest author leads to a respected expert, a brief online reference leads to an entire website. Award-winning teacher Nancy Barile (n.d.) created a list of ten reliable online sources that provide free information about a broad range of topics related to education.

1. **ReadWriteThink (www.readwritethink.org):** This is the National Council of Teachers of English's website; it contains resources for reading and English language arts instruction.

2. **PhET (https://phet.colorado.edu/en/teaching-resources):** For educators looking for ways to teach science, mathematics, engineering, and technology, this University of Colorado Boulder site offers interactive simulations.

3. **Resources for Teachers From Scholastic (www.scholastic.com /teachers/teaching-tools/home.html):** This Scholastic site contains a huge variety of activities, lists, and guides for books for grades K–8 students.

4. **Stanford History Education Group (https://sheg.stanford.edu):** The Stanford History Education Group site features resources about addressing central historical questions as well as primary documents tailored to student reading levels.

5. **PBS LearningMedia (https://pbslearningmedia.org):** PBS LearningMedia has frequently updated interactive lessons in a variety of content areas.

6. **Epic! (www.getepic.com/educators):** The Epic! digital reading platform gives educators access to thousands of ebooks, including books written in Spanish; it also offers learning videos and quizzes.

7. **EDSITEment (https://edsitement.neh.gov):** EDSITEment features humanities-focused content, including lessons, and the opportunity to get student resources and interactive materials.

8. **Illuminations (https://illuminations.nctm.org):** Created by the National Council of Teachers of Mathematics, this site features lesson plans, activities, games, and interactive tools for students at all levels.

9. **Learning for Justice (www.learningforjustice.org):** Learning for Justice, formerly known as Teaching Tolerance, focuses on equity and social justice. The site offers materials that can supplement curriculum to ensure that classrooms are inclusive, respectful, and welcoming.

10. **National Geographic Society (www.nationalgeographic.org/society /education-resources):** The National Geographic Society features activities, lessons, and even entire units that teachers can use or adapt.

Closer to home are colleagues who may have resources that will help if you let these colleagues know you're looking. From the intern conducting a survey on student reflection to the principal working on a doctoral degree about the impact of grades on learning, what you need might already be in the building. Let's say you and I share an interest in encouraging students to take a more active role in assessing their own work, and we think a student-friendly rubric will help. Using some of the methods described earlier in this section, we collaborate on collecting information, including asking colleagues for suggestions.

A colleague recommends *How to Create and Use Rubrics for Formative Assessment and Grading* by Susan M. Brookhart, published in 2013. The book becomes a hinge point for us as we go back to research on rubrics from the 1980s that Brookhart builds on, and we go forward to use of rubrics for self-assessment.

In the first chapter, there is an eye-opening passage:

> To write or select rubrics, teachers need to focus on the criteria by which learning will be assessed. This focus on what you intend students to learn rather than what you intend to teach actually helps improve instruction. . . . Really good rubrics help teachers avoid confusing the task or activity with the learning goal, and therefore confusing completion of the task with learning. Rubrics help keep teachers focused on criteria, not tasks. (Brookhart, 2013, p. 11)

This might be the most important piece of information that we collect. We are also intrigued that Brookhart (2013) thinks the same rubric should be used consistently and continuously over the course of a task and over a set of related tasks. Brookhart (2013) makes it clear that the research is in on the impact of rubrics on student learning:

Effective rubrics show students how they will know to what extent their performance passes muster on each criterion of importance, and if used formatively can also show students what their next steps should be to enhance the quality of their performance. This claim is backed by research at all grade levels and in different disciplines. (p. 12)

This passage also gives us another eye-opening moment. Brookhart (2013) proposes here that the usefulness of rubrics is not just in assessing the final product but in sharing information with students while they are working on a piece of writing, which will help them revise.

The role rubrics can play in guiding revision is at the heart of an interview with Vicki Spandel (Peha, 2018). Spandel was a major player in the 1980s work on rubrics, but her thinking about the purpose of rubrics shifted dramatically. Because of a colleague's offhand comment that a rubric was a "blueprint for revision," Spandel realized that the real purpose of her work all along had been teaching students to revise—formative rather than summative assessment: "The answer had been right there in front of us—and from that moment my workshops, my writing, everything changed" (Peha, 2018). You and I realize this is what Susan Brookhart (2013) has in mind when she writes that rubrics, "if used formatively, can also show students what their next steps should be to enhance the quality of their performance" (p. 12). In classroom action research, one thing leads to another.

Implement the Plan and Evaluate the Results

When classroom action research shifts from collecting information and developing a plan to actually using research in the classroom with students, there are a number of things to consider.

- Has the question or problem that launched the action research changed? If so, what question has the research actually answered?

- What new materials and methods are needed to implement the plan?

- What elements can be built into implementation that will provide information about the plan's impact on student learning? What evidence will show whether the plan has been successful?

It's a good idea to keep things simple when trying something new with students. In the case of the student-friendly rubric, we need a task that taps into elements of the course that students are already familiar with, and we want the task to be engaging enough that students are likely to do it as well as possible. The example I want to share is called the *image project*. I developed it to use with secondary students, but you can adapt it for primary students as well. The project is simple: students each pick an image that matters to them and, in no more than 250 words, explain why it matters. In figure 3.1, you will find a list of steps students need to take to complete this task. This is a list of steps that students need to keep in mind while working on the assignment. A checklist like this is used for guidance, not for assessment. The checklist also helps teachers differentiate between process steps and learning goals so evaluation can clearly focus on progress toward achievement of learning goals.

☐ Find an image that matters to you and record where and when you found it.

☐ Draft an explanation of why the image matters.

☐ Do background research about the image—when, where, and by whom it was taken—and record your sources.

☐ Analyze the image much as you would a literary text.

☐ Combine your explanation, information, and analysis into a caption (maximum 250 words).

☐ Use the formative rubric to guide revision of your caption.

☐ Meet with your peer feedback group to focus on language and voice.

☐ Create a document that includes your image, caption, and sources.

☐ Post your document to a class website or blog.

☐ Write a reflection on both the process and the completed project.

FIGURE 3.1: Process checklist for the image project.

*Visit **go.SolutionTree.com/teacherefficacy** for a free reproducible version of this figure.*

Once the process list is done, it's safe to go ahead with the rubric, which will focus not on steps but on learning goals. The categories and the criteria in the Meets Expectations column of the rubric (figure 3.2, page 50) should come straight from grade-level or course learning goals that have already been shared with students; this way, the students are familiar with the language and focus of the goals. Wording of the criteria in the Needs Development and Exceeds Expectations columns should also be familiar to students, drawing on the language you and colleagues already use when speaking with students or writing comments on their work.

Figure 3.2 provides a sample of a rubric for an eleventh-grade image project.

Category	Needs development	Meets expectations	Exceeds expectations
Process	Provide vague feedback to peers. Make superficial revisions that do not meet expectations.	Move effectively through the writing process with careful attention to inquiry and research, drafting and revision, and editing and review.	Provide detailed and insightful feedback to peers. Use feedback to revise with the goal of exceeding expectations for all criteria.
Analysis	State the personal relevance of an image without explaining what gives it impact.	Interpret the meaning of an image, identifying and explaining the strategies and techniques that give it impact.	Provide a nuanced interpretation of an image, identifying sophisticated strategies and techniques that give it impact.
Language and voice	Use generic words and basic sentence structures to present information and opinion.	Use precise word choices, sentence variety, and figurative language to convey meaning and attitude.	Display a clear and individual voice that conveys meaning and attitude.
Conventions of print	Proofread to correct some errors. Include a list of references that is incomplete or incorrectly formatted.	Proofread to correct most errors. Include a list of references.	Demonstrate mastery of conventions of print and source citation.
Collaboration	Come to peer feedback sessions unprepared.	Take and share responsibility for collaborative work.	Deal positively with praise, setbacks, and criticism.
Reflection	Comment briefly on the work of others and on your own process.	Comment thoughtfully on the work of others and on your own process.	Comment insightfully and in detail on the work of others and on your own process.

FIGURE 3.2: Sample image project rubric for secondary students that includes collaboration and reflection.

*Visit **go.SolutionTree.com/teacherefficacy** for a free reproducible version of this figure.*

There are four ways to use the sample rubric with a task such as the image project.

1. **Use the rubric to introduce the task so students know from the start what the criteria for success will be:** When you are working with a team on action research, you can hold a joint meeting with students to introduce the task. Consider the plan a success when students are able to begin work with few follow-up questions.

2. **Ask students to use the rubric to provide feedback in peer response groups:** Visit the groups to observe how students are using the rubric and to help with any questions or issues. You and team members can use this step to visit one another's classrooms and listen to one another's students providing feedback. Consider the plan a success when students use the language of the rubric as they comment on one another's works in progress.

3. **Use the rubric to provide formative feedback once students have had a chance to revise based on peer response:** In this way, you and your team members can use the rubric on samples of works in progress from all your classes just to be sure that you are using the rubric consistently. Consider the plan a success when the rubric captures most of the comments you feel need to be made on the students' works in progress.

4. **Ask students to use the rubric to self-assess once they complete their projects:** By this time, students should be well acquainted with the learning goals and the language in which they are described. You and your team members can study students' self-assessments from several perspectives: what percentage of students are meeting expectations, which categories on the final projects still need development, which categories have students exceeding expectations, and what implications these findings have for further research. Consider the plan a success when students' assessments are in alignment with your own.

Repeat the Process

If the results of implementing the plan are ambiguous, you will want to quite literally repeat the process. It's a good idea to begin by asking for student feedback. You can inquire generally about the project as well as solicit feedback specifically on the rubric.

- What did you like about the project?
- What would you change?
- Did the rubric help you in these situations?
    - Understanding how to meet expectations
    - Giving feedback to other students
    - Self-assessing your own work
- What would make the rubric more useful to you?

If the results are emphatically positive, repeating the process means using a similar rubric with a similar task to confirm the results. At this point, you will have some definite ideas about what works and why. This is a useful time to do some reflective writing that you can then share with members of an action-research team. After that, you might want to consider sharing your work with other colleagues in the same grade level or content area. In a K–12 workshop format, you all could take on the additional challenge of collaboratively walking teachers at multiple grade levels and content areas through the process checklist and formative rubric. The details will differ, but the underlying concepts will be the same. For a K–12 workshop, you should offer samples of process checklists and rubrics at both secondary and primary levels and in multiple content areas.

Figure 3.3 provides a sample process checklist for a fifth-grade science experiment.

☐ Form a group.

☐ Select a question, discuss it, and decide on a hypothesis.

☐ Design an experiment to test your hypothesis.

☐ Assign tasks and gather appropriate tools and materials, including safety gear.

☐ Decide on a method to record and display the results.

☐ Conduct the experiment, and record the results.

☐ Display and discuss the results.

☐ Discuss possible explanations for the results, including human error.

FIGURE 3.3: Sample process checklist for a fifth-grade science experiment.

*Visit **go.SolutionTree.com/teacherefficacy** for a free reproducible version of this figure.*

In a workshop setting, a rubric with only the middle column filled in can help you make the point that the Meets Expectations column needs to be drawn from grade-level or course goals. You can leave the other columns blank so participants will collaboratively, and with your guidance, fill the columns with specific criteria written in student-friendly language.

Figure 3.4 provides a sample of such a rubric for a fifth-grade science experiment.

Learning goal: Design and conduct scientific investigations to understand that there may be more than one explanation for results.			
	Attempts goal	Meets goal	Exceeds goal
Questions		Identify questions that can be answered through scientific investigations.	
Tools and techniques		Use appropriate tools and techniques to gather, analyze, and interpret data.	
Use of evidence		Use evidence to develop descriptions, explanations, predictions, and models.	
Connections made		Think critically and logically to make valid connections between evidence and explanations.	

FIGURE 3.4: Sample rubric in progress for a fifth-grade science experiment.

*Visit **go.SolutionTree.com/teacherefficacy** for a free reproducible version of this figure.*

The Meets Expectations column drawn from grade-level or course goals can also be used in a two-column format, like the sample in figure 3.5 (page 54), for reflection and goal setting.

Conducting a workshop gives you an opportunity to step up as a teacher leader and contribute the results of classroom action research to the school community as a whole. A good idea is a good idea across grade levels and content areas.

It takes time and thought to develop a rubric that goes beyond "too little of that" and "lots of this," but the process accomplishes two important things: (1) it distinguishes between the steps of a process and progress toward achievement of learning goals, and (2) it provides a clear, concise way to share information that helps students succeed. Classroom action research makes it possible for teacher leaders to look at students' needs from more than one perspective. The opportunity for multiple perspectives is active in demonstration lessons as well.

Learning goals for a science experiment	Science experiment reflections and goals Use the space provided in this chart to reflect on your participation in the experiment and your goals for the next one.
Identify questions that can be answered through scientific investigations.	
Use appropriate tools and techniques to gather, analyze, and interpret data.	
Use evidence to develop descriptions, explanations, predictions, and models.	
Think critically and logically to make valid connections between evidence and explanations.	

FIGURE 3.5: Sample self-assessment chart for a fifth-grade science experiment with space for reflection and goal setting.

*Visit **go.SolutionTree.com/teacherefficacy** for a free reproducible version of this figure.*

DEMONSTRATION LESSONS

When you invite colleagues into your classroom to see what you're up to, and when you encourage colleagues to invite each other into their classrooms for demonstration of a concept or approach, the classroom becomes a place where teachers can learn from one another. In this way, the classroom serves the dual role of improving teacher practice and improving student learning. Sometimes the most effective way to share a new instructional strategy or method with the school community is to show rather than tell. Besides the benefits of sharing a promising new idea with others, demonstration lessons offer everyone chances to see new perspectives and potentially further improve their strategies.

It's easy to find information about formal evaluative observation and teacher observation as elements of peer coaching. In these observation settings, the teacher to be observed is the object of structured study and feedback. But when teachers observe other teachers to learn about their own practice—what's working and what could be improved—the observed teacher is the subject of professional learning that can have immense value. Catherine Trinkle (2019) is an instructional coach at Avon High School in Avon, Indiana. In her article "With Peer Visits, Teachers See for Themselves

How to Improve Practice," she discusses what she learned from a 2018 survey about what U.S. teachers want from professional learning:

> Teachers want professional learning to be personalized and responsive to their unique needs in the classroom (Trinkle, 2018). Those who had no influence in determining the content of professional learning were more likely to leave teaching than those who felt they had a great deal of influence over the content of the professional learning in their schools (Trinkle, 2018). Teachers who were able to observe other teachers were also more likely to remain in the profession. (Trinkle, 2019, p. 1)

These findings are echoed whenever discussion of teacher observation touches on teachers' observing other teachers as an important source of professional learning. In an article for *Education World* titled "Teachers Observing Teachers: A Professional Development Tool for Every School," Michele Israel (n.d.) interviews nearly a dozen professional learning experts from all over the United States, and they all agree that the impact of teachers' observing teachers is positive and powerful. One of the interviewees, University of Pennsylvania education researcher and former teacher Cristi Alberino, emphasizes that teachers "should use one another for professional development" (Israel, n.d.). Alberino provides the example that "a teacher struggling with classroom management can improve his or her [or their] skills by observing a peer in a safe and inclusive learning environment" (Israel, n.d.).

Dennis Sparks, former executive director of the National Staff Development Council (now Learning Forward), emphasizes the importance of a collegial school culture where administrators trust teachers and teachers trust each other. Sparks says, "It's a risky thing to have your professional practice scrutinized by colleagues" (Israel, n.d.). "Most important to effective teacher observation is that it be student-focused. The emphasis needs to be on how things can be done differently in the classroom to ensure that students succeed academically, [adds] Sparks" (Israel, n.d.).

Teachers' participation in peer visits and demonstration lessons has the added benefit that students observe their teachers working together. Jennifer Gonzalez (2013), in her *Cult of Pedagogy* blog post "Open Your Door: Why We Need to See Each Other Teach," comments on why this matters:

> Something powerful happens when students see their teachers together. You become larger than the sum of your parts, stronger not only in number, but because this simple show of cooperation tells them you are united, which is an important message to send to kids. In the same way that children feel more secure when their parents are getting along, students feel something similar when they see us support each other.

You can get started on demonstrations by doing one yourself. Then invite a colleague to teach a lesson with your students. As the experts have noted, watching a colleague teach concepts and strategies to your students in the classroom can be eye opening. With any luck, a few demonstrations will open the door to more, perhaps a daylong exchange involving all teachers in a grade level or content area.

Scaling up from a demonstration in your classroom or the one next door to a demonstration involving all teachers in a given grade level or content area is a great opportunity for teacher leaders to influence, support, and renew the school community. What follows is a list of steps you might take in order to expand access to demonstrations.

1. Check in with administrators to make sure they are on board with the idea, and ask for their support.

2. Make demonstration lessons the topic of a department or grade-level meeting. What are they? Why are they a good idea? What does one look like? Provide a mini-demonstration as a sample to generate understanding and interest.

3. Pair up colleagues who are already comfortable with each other to participate in an exchange of classroom visits. In some cases, colleagues can bring their students along. In others, coverage will be needed. You can provide some of this yourself, ask for volunteers to donate a free period to cover a class, and, if needed, request support from administrators to bring in a substitute.

4. Ask for volunteers to teach demonstration lessons to a small group of colleagues so the experience is shared and participants have the added benefit of talking it over. The intention here is not to have every member of the grade level or content area participate but to generate interest in a demo day that would include everyone. You can limit participation to those who are free at the same time, or you can figure out a schedule for coverage.

5. Ask administrators for support so all teachers in a grade level or content area can participate in a demo day. Providing coverage so everyone who wants to participate is free to do so clearly sends the message that teacher collaboration is important to administrators. Figure 3.6 shows what the roster might look like for a pair of demonstration lessons focused on science projects. The roster for a

Time	Name of host, topic, and observers	Class, supervision, or duty to be covered	Coverage provider (substitute, intern)
8:30–9:20 a.m.	Host 1, "Build a River Model" Teacher A Teacher B Teacher C	Welcome desk	Intern
9:25–10:15 a.m.	Host 2, "Make a Wind Gauge" Teacher D Teacher E Teacher F	Recess Language arts	Intern Substitute

FIGURE 3.6: Sample roster for an exchange of demonstration lessons.

large grade level or content area would have more sessions and more teachers at each session, and it might be structured so teachers have the chance to sign up for more than one demonstration.

Demonstration lessons allow colleagues to get acquainted with materials and methods that teacher leaders find worthwhile. And they allow colleagues to observe how a classroom is set up; what expectations are in place; how the teacher interacts with students; and what use the teacher makes of body language, humor, references to current events, and so on to interact with students. But the ultimate goal is a collaborative culture in which colleagues feel comfortable visiting one another's classrooms. Whether organizing a day of demonstration lessons or covering a class so one teacher is free to visit another, teacher leaders can encourage and support powerful professional learning in the classroom.

SUMMARY

The goal of this chapter has been to open classroom doors and give colleagues opportunities to learn from one another by collaborating on action research at the classroom level and taking on the risk of sharing who they are as teachers. All members of the school community benefit when trust is high. I couldn't sum up the benefits of this level of collaborative action research and demonstration better than Jennifer Gonzalez (2013) does:

Watching another person deeply involved in the work they're trained for helps you get to know them on a completely different level. And though we work together, we usually follow parallel, rather than intersecting lines. We rarely ever actually see each other teach. And it's a shame, because every time I've observed a colleague, my admiration for them has grown, and each time, I felt a little closer to them. This is something we could use more of in every workplace—educational or not.

Chapter 4 explores the many ways that teacher leaders can use professional learning based on classroom action research and demonstration lessons to renew instruction and improve student learning.

NEXT STEPS FOR RESEARCH AND PROFESSIONAL LEARNING TO MEET STUDENT NEEDS

The following tool details some steps you can take to experiment with strategies for taking on research and professional learning to meet student needs. For each step, note the date you tried it and reflect on how it went. *What did you do? How did it go? What would you change? What's next?* There are spaces available at the end for you to plan additional steps you can take toward teacher leadership.

Next Steps Tried	Date Tried	Reflection
Invite a colleague to observe or participate in a classroom activity that engages your students in learning, and ask for feedback.		
Ask a colleague to invite you to observe or participate in a classroom activity and offer positive and constructive feedback.		
Design and conduct a classroom action research project with your colleague. Study and discuss the impact on students.		

page 1 of 2

Ask a colleague to join you in organizing a series of demonstration lessons for your grade level or content area.				

Renewal and Improvement of Instruction and Student Learning

In 1992, James Moffett and Betty Jane Wagner were seething over the fact that curriculum and textbook production as a profit-making industry still held students and teachers in some U.S. states hostage. In their book *Student-Centered Language Arts, K–12*, they advised teachers to cut themselves loose from ready-made materials and celebrated the growing number of districts that were "making their curriculum guidelines more independent of commercial materials" (Moffett & Wagner, 1992, p. 6).

This guidance still has relevance for teacher leaders, who can wield much influence from the classroom when it comes to renewing and improving instruction. Teachers should develop and adapt what they value, what they teach, and how they assess learning to meet the needs of students actually in the classroom. In an article titled "The Obvious Path to Better Professional Development," educational consultant Mike Schmoker (2021) details Brockton High School's ascent from placing near the bottom of Massachusetts school rankings to exemplifying what schools can accomplish through curriculum that is independent of commercial materials and frees teachers to attend to the specific needs of students they know well. He writes, "The transformation of this enormous, diverse, high-poverty school began in 1999 with a coordinated effort to build a coherent, teacher-generated curriculum" (Schmoker, 2021). A major focus of the curriculum work was integration of the fundamental skills of reading and writing, thinking and reasoning across grade levels and content areas, and training to help teachers renew instruction.

But the transformation didn't stop there. One of the many parts teacher leaders can play is school leadership team member. At Brockton High School, the leadership team committed the time necessary to be a frequent presence in classrooms, providing feedback and targeted training that helped teachers align their day-to-day practice with the curriculum they had written. Some teachers resisted the intensive follow-up until the first-year results were in and everyone could see the huge leap in achievement that Brockton's four thousand students had made.

In this chapter, I get into the specifics of how teacher-written curricula can address specific needs, can do so without overreaching, and can include follow-up that is both honest and respectful and has the power to renew and improve instruction and student learning. I discuss assessment's enormous potential to improve student learning and numerous ways teacher leaders can ensure their effectiveness for both themselves and their colleagues. Last, I explain how teacher leaders are instrumental in solving the inevitable problems that arise over the course of a school year and keeping student learning on track.

TEACHER-WRITTEN CURRICULUM

A good, hardworking curriculum serves as a linchpin for grade levels, content areas, and the school community as a whole. The curriculum links local and state or provincial goals and informs students and families of what is especially relevant and important about each grade level and content area. It expresses fundamental principles of education in clear and welcoming language and provides the guidance teachers need to collaborate toward helping all students achieve success.

Teacher leaders can help spearhead these important considerations, being particularly attentive to the elements of an effective curriculum, following up on the curriculum in practice, and heeding student feedback.

Elements of an Effective Curriculum

As a new teacher, I witnessed a major shift in curriculum writing, from scope and sequence to content and performance standards. The scope-and-sequence approach maps the content students will be taught. The standards-based approach, which dates back to the early 1980s, establishes priorities for what students should know and be able to do (Depka, 2022; Schimmer, Hillman, & Stalets, 2018). Instead of covering all the items in the scope and sequence, this approach encourages teachers to limit the number of topics students encounter so they work with the remaining topics in greater depth. It encourages acquisition of skills over memorization of facts, acknowledging that students live in a world with almost limitless access to information but that they need the ability to deepen their understanding of that world through critical thinking, problem solving, collaboration, and so on.

About the same time this major shift was gaining momentum, Grant Wiggins pioneered the use of essential questions in an educational setting during his work with the Coalition of Essential Schools (McKenzie, 2016). Wiggins and Jay McTighe (1998) explain that the idea is to focus learning on students' development of nuanced responses to genuine, open-ended questions, instead of on correct responses to narrow questions that have only one right answer. Education editor and writer Jamie McKenzie (2016) clarifies how essential questions can transform curriculum design:

> These questions often kindle curiosity and provide the driving force for a unit lasting several weeks or months. When first introduced by the Coalition [of Essential Schools], a single question might serve to organize learning for an entire year. [An example of such a question is] "What makes people want to explore?"

Wiggins and McTighe (1998) assert that students learn content and skills better when they can use their developing knowledge and skills to generate an in-depth response to an intriguing question. This approach continues to guide teachers to foster curiosity in students and encourage students to deepen their thinking. A helpful explainer from Chalk (2021) describes the characteristics of essential questions:

1. **Are open-ended:** Do not have a single, final, and correct answer.
2. **Are thought-provoking and intellectually engaging:** Often sparking discussion and debate.
3. **Require higher-order thinking:** Cannot be effectively answered by recall alone—analysis, inference, evaluation, and prediction.
4. **Develop transferable ideas:** Across subject or unit topics, as well as other disciplines.
5. **Spark additional questions:** Inquisitive-based learning is a crucial feature.
6. **Use support and justification:** Claim, support, conclusion—not just a singular answer.
7. **Evolve with time:** Questions revisited, new approaches taken, and new ideas brought to the table.

In a classic article for *Horace*, education journalist Kathleen Cushman (1989) proposes questions that could apply to every subject area:

- From whose viewpoint are we seeing or reading or hearing? From what angle or perspective?

- How do we know when we know? What's the evidence, and how reliable is it?

- How are things, events, or people connected to each other? What is the cause and what is the effect? How do they fit together?

- What's new and what's old? Have we run across this idea before?

- So what? Why does it matter? What does it all mean?

An effective essential question is direct and engaging. A second grader would have some thoughts about it, and it would seem worthwhile to a high school junior. An example from Cushman (1989) concerns the world of plants: "Do stems of germinating seedlings always grow upwards and roots downwards?" This is a question that invites students to go beyond their initial response to find out more through relevant sources and hands-on experimentation. The process of developing a more complex answer to this question would lead students beyond the ability to succeed on a test to a genuine grasp of concepts that are memorable and relevant in the larger world.

This thinking about standards and essential questions leads directly into the actual how-to of writing curriculum. The curriculum-writing guidelines provided in the following list are a distillation of twenty-five years of my own experience using, revising, and generating curriculum. A reproducible version of these guidelines is available on page 81.

- Select learning goals that are truly essential (right at the core of the grade level or content area).

- Limit the number of learning goals so each one can be woven throughout the curriculum, giving students many opportunities to practice and, over time, achieve enduring mastery of each goal.

- Students learn best when they feel known and have a sense of belonging. Make getting to know students' interests and needs a universal priority, and identify methods and materials in the curriculum that are relevant to students.

- Focus the curriculum not just on teaching but on helping students learn how to learn.

- Include performance assessments that invite students to demonstrate their mastery of learning goals. Students can demonstrate what they have achieved in many ways: a portfolio with reflective commentary, an account of the process of designing and completing a multistep project, and a wide variety of other projects and performances.

Writing or revising a curriculum is a process that starts with broad thinking about what students need to know and be able to do and gradually becomes focused on concepts, methods, materials, activities, and assessments that will provide structure and support for teaching and learning. Robert J. Marzano's notion of the guaranteed and viable curriculum has a direct bearing here, since it emphasizes that all students in the school should receive access to the same high-quality curriculum, and that curriculum should be focused so it's possible for teachers to deliver it in the time they have available (Marzano, Warrick, Rains, & DuFour, 2018). Marzano and his colleagues (2018) also point out that teachers must work together to answer the question of what they want students to know, and that the curriculum they create must exist in easily accessible documents. Angela Di Michele Lalor's (2022) article distilling her work on a framework called Curriculum That Matters identifies five key elements that align a curriculum with a school or district's vision and mission and make the curriculum relevant to teachers and students.

1. Teach practices as well as content and engage students "in authentic tasks that allow them to see how practices are used in the real world" (Lalor, 2022).

2. Promote deep thinking with "multistep, complex tasks that take place over time, involve individual and group work, and provide opportunities for feedback and revision" (Lalor, 2022).

3. Organize units of study around "essential questions and big ideas that examine the SEL [social-emotional learning] competencies" (Lalor, 2022).

4. Provide opportunities for civic engagement in the classroom community to help students "develop human and social capital helpful to achieving their goals" (Lalor, 2022).

5. Offer respect to each student, and integrate that respect into curriculum with "texts and resources that include characters and people of different cultures, races, ethnicities, religions, abilities, classes, sexual orientation, and gender identities—and that are written by authors from these diverse groups" (Lalor, 2022).

In addition to identifying these five essential elements of a curriculum that matters, Lalor (2022) makes two crucial points about the impact of teacher-generated curriculum on both teachers and students. First, writing or revising a curriculum helps teachers clarify "what they are teaching and why" and provides opportunities to discuss and understand practices that will make the curriculum meaningful in the classroom (Lalor, 2022). And second, a curriculum that "honors who they are" has increased potential to engage students in learning and developing the skills necessary to make decisions about "their own pathways in life" (Lalor, 2022). When teachers have input on what to prioritize within their grade levels and content areas, they can also help ensure that they are able to teach the content rather than merely cover it (Marzano et al., 2018).

A specific example from my own experience of the impact curriculum writing can have on teachers and students involves a tenth-grade English curriculum that was sorely in need of revision. The group charged with making this happen was composed of teachers with various levels of experience teaching tenth grade and writing curriculum. But they all participated as teacher leaders in the process of developing a collaborative vision of the curriculum, designing units of study, reviewing one another's work, presenting the draft to colleagues for comment, and, ultimately, seeking approval from the board of education. Each member of the group contributed in roughly equal measure to all these phases of the process. We began by taking time to talk about how our expectations of students had changed and what was important to us as educators and inhabitants of the planet. As a result of this discussion, the tenth-grade curriculum evolved into a multifaceted exploration of culture. It primarily focused on world cultures, but we defined *culture* broadly enough to include the culture of classical Greece and microcultures within our own, such as the culture of disenfranchisement and the culture of youth. We brainstormed characteristics of tenth graders that are distinct from those of younger and older students and identified courses in other subject areas that would offer natural connections to a cultural focus, including history, sociology, anthropology, psychology, art, and music. As our vision for the course began to develop, we agreed on several crucial points that would guide our work.

- Provide a proactive approach to teenage students' essential needs to be known and to be valued, which will intensify as the high school population expands.

- Build students' understanding of other people in diverse settings and situations.

- Increase a disposition in students to empathize and feel compassion for others.

- Develop students' individual purpose in life through a sense of connection with the world.

- Help students see that they can change the world in small increments through a day-to-day focus on possibilities.

- Encourage students to develop and articulate their own ideas and beliefs.

Development of the tenth-grade curriculum was an exciting process. Once the curriculum was up and running, both students and teachers expressed great satisfaction with the curriculum's relevance to the real world and with the rich opportunities the curriculum offered to connect classical culture with contemporary culture and to make connections between subject areas.

Units of study within the larger curriculum can be formatted as a chart, like the one in figure 4.1; this allows students and families to more easily see connections between the unit and the curriculum as a whole. The process of constructing the chart makes the focus and purpose of the unit of study clearer to teachers as well.

Focus and purpose of the unit of study:				
Essential question:				
Key features	Topics	Core concepts	Learning goals	Notes
Primary resources				
Supplemental materials				
Formative activities				
Performance tasks				

FIGURE 4.1: Template for charting a unit of study.

*Visit **go.SolutionTree.com/teacherefficacy** for a free reproducible version of this figure.*

Let's say you're working on a unit of study for that tenth-grade curriculum. You want your students to encounter individuals from different cultures and grapple with how cultural background creates diversity at the same time that people have fundamental human qualities in common. To underscore this duality, you could ask your students to experiment with multiple genres as they write about what they are learning. Instead of making separate analytical and creative assignments, you could ask students to write vignettes based on their research about world cultures and integrate them into a research project. The goals would be to help students use their own thinking and writing to more deeply understand the connections between culture and individual and to share their understanding with other students in multiple ways. Figure 4.2 provides a filled-out example of such a chart.

Participation in curriculum work is stimulating and rewarding. Curriculum writing gives teacher leaders a chance to think out loud, share and learn successful teaching strategies, generate and connect ideas, and collaboratively create an enduring contribution to the grade level or content area and to the school and district.

The Case for Follow-Up

Let's return to the model school from the chapter introduction (page 61), Brockton High School, and take a closer look at the initial resistance from some teachers when they realized that writing a coherent curriculum for the entire school was just the beginning. Their process of professional learning would also include classroom visits to follow up and provide additional training, as needed. Teachers will say, "You're always welcome," and "I want you to see what we're doing," and they will mean it, but classroom visits can be disconcerting, especially if they are unannounced. They can of course make teachers feel put on the spot, but visits can also feel uncomfortable for another reason, one that is seldom discussed. Jennifer Gonzalez (2013) describes the reason:

> Alone with my students, I'm a different person: I let my guard down in a way that I never do with co-workers, even people I'm comfortable with. My students get the most relaxed, funniest side of me, the side I'm not sure my colleagues would appreciate or approve of.

Yet there is no better way to support teachers in implementing the curriculum they have written than to provide the detailed feedback that can be generated only by devoting many hours and much thought to classroom visits. While such visits often come from administrators, teacher leaders have the capacity to understand and commiserate with colleagues' initial discomfort. And teacher leaders can grasp follow-up's importance in fully achieving teacher-generated curriculum that renews instruction and student learning. Providing follow-up as a team effort that includes

Focus and purpose of the unit of study: Build an understanding of other people in diverse settings and situations. Increase a disposition to empathize and feel compassion for others. Encourage students to develop and articulate their own ideas and beliefs.

Essential question: What makes us who we are?

Key features	Topics	Core concepts	Learning goals	Notes
Primary resources	*The House on Mango Street*, Cisneros *A Summer Life*, Soto *In the Time of the Butterflies*, Alvarez	Private lives may depart from public expectations.	Analyze and interpret how an author's use of dialogue and detail reveals perspective.	If time is short, invite students to read with a partner (one book read by both and one read by each, then discussed).
Supplemental materials	Poems from Poetry Out Loud related to each student's cultural background	Students can use the form of a poem to understand meaning and how to read it out loud.	Memorize and perform the selected poem, modulating pace and volume to convey meaning.	Students who are reluctant to perform in public should have the option of reading their poem out loud.
Formative activities	Writing vignettes about growing up with a specific cultural perspective	Participation in a writing group helps writers hone their work and learn new techniques from the work of others.	Assume shared responsibility for collaborative work.	Set aside regular and significant time for writing groups, as the benefits for students are significant.
Performance tasks	Weaving the vignettes into a thoughtful and well-supported response to the essential question	An initial response to the essential question may change over the course of the unit of study.	Convey information and ideas with authority and originality.	If there is time, invite students to celebrate their work by reading the work of four or five others and writing a note of appreciation.

FIGURE 4.2: Sample unit-of-study chart.

administrators, specialists, and teacher leaders makes it possible to reach the full potential of curriculum work yet respect some teachers' need to adjust to frequent classroom visits. Just like the demonstration lessons described in chapter 3 (page 43), finding the benefits in classroom visits requires a collaborative culture and trust.

In an Edutopia article titled "How to Lead With Empathy," Paige Tutt (2022) reports on practices that normalize and de-stress classroom visits. These guidelines can be shared both with the members of the leadership team making the visits and with the teachers receiving the follow-up.

- Leave the laptop or notebook behind, and make the visit empty-handed.

- Take time to ask students about the assignment or sit in with a small group.

- Follow up on the visit with a comment or note of encouragement and appreciation.

- Keep track of time spent to ensure that it's about equal for each teacher over the course of the year.

All of us benefit from a compassionate and honest mixture of affirmation of our strengths and acknowledgment of areas that could use more work. Like the classroom action research of chapter 3 (page 43), teacher-generated curriculum creates a dynamic cycle of information gathering, experimentation, and evaluation that continually improves instruction and student learning. The work will never be done, and the goal is not perfection but continual improvement. The example of Brockton High School is a reminder of how much we educators can accomplish when we work together to improve. We need to trust each other to do the best we can on any given day and to want to become the best versions of ourselves. Trust turns obligations into opportunities; trust is precious, and it is something teacher leaders can consciously and generously provide for colleagues.

Student Feedback

Teacher leaders devote a lot of time and thought to understanding how students are doing, and it's important that they not overlook one of the best sources of information: the students themselves. What students know about how they're doing and how we're doing represents a wealth of information. Students need opportunities to reflect on class activities and school programs, to self-assess their progress, and to evaluate their classes, their programs, and the teachers who work with them.

You can request regular feedback about how things are going in class using questions such as those in figure 4.3. Paying close attention to what students have to say will help you adjust content to meet their needs and interests and motivate and guide your continued growth as a teacher leader.

Your feedback is important to me. **Please respond to the following questions.**	
Participation: Do you participate in class discussions? What have you learned from listening to other students?	
Response: What have you learned from peer feedback? What could you do to give even more helpful responses to others?	
Achievement: What are you proudest of, and what do you see as your area of greatest growth?	
Needs: What concerns or questions do you have about your work? Would a student-teacher conference help?	
Suggestions: What is one thing I can do to make the class more useful, meaningful, or enjoyable?	
What question did I forget to ask?	

FIGURE 4.3: State-of-the-student report.

Visit go.SolutionTree.com/teacherefficacy for a free reproducible version of this figure.

In *The Wraparound Guide: How to Gather Student Voice, Build Community Partnerships, and Cultivate Hope*, Leigh Colburn and Linda Beggs (2020) combine many years of teacher leadership at many levels—classroom, administration, and consultation. Their overarching concern is the impact of agency and voice on students' capacity to be whole and well. The book includes a student feedback form used to gather information about the impact of a program called the Wraparound Services Center, which provides support to students in a number of ways. I have always found that students appreciate opportunities to share their experiences and to know their voices are heard. The student feedback form in figure 4.4 (page 72) seeks information about students' level of participation in the program as well as their feedback on the program, and it also offers an invitation for students to contribute as volunteers.

Students,

We have had an exciting year in our Wraparound Services Center (WSC). We hope you have come to see us and taken advantage of some of the services we are providing. Please help us improve by completing this form to give us some information on what we are doing well and where we might need to do better as we plan for the next school year. Include any ideas or suggestions you have for the Wraparound Services Center.

Have you attended our Wraparound Services Center?

- Yes
- No

If you answered *Yes* to the previous question, what services or support did you receive? (Please check all that apply.)

- Tutoring
- Mentoring or personal support
- Graduation planning (alternative scheduling, academic advice, and so on)
- College and career services (YouScience, military recruitment, SAT or ACT prep, college information, scholarship assistance, and so on)
- Personal needs (food pantry, clothes closet, housing assistance, and so on)
- Support groups (yoga, stress management, anger management, self-esteem, and so on)

Please tell us your thoughts on the WSC.

What is going well?

Has the WSC been of assistance to you? If so, how?

Is there something we need to improve? If so, what?

Do you have any ideas you would like to share with us? If so, what are they?

If you could tell another school or another student something about the WSC, what would you tell them?

In what ways, if any, would you be interested in becoming more involved in the WSC? (Please check all that apply.)

- ☐ I would be interested in volunteering my time in the clothes closet.
- ☐ I would be interested in serving on the student board of directors.
- ☐ I would be interested in serving as a WSC tour guide.
- ☐ I would be interested in assisting with service projects related to the WSC.

Contact information is optional but appreciated—especially if you checked any of the boxes above

Your name: _____

Email address: _____ Phone number: _____

Source: Colburn & Beggs, 2020, p. 194.

FIGURE 4.4: Student feedback form.

Students get to see a lot of teachers over their years in school, and they learn to read us well. Student feedback is valuable schoolwide for refining class and course content, improving teaching practice, and increasing the quality of school programs and students' access to them. I think we sometimes try so hard to achieve a specific objective that we inadvertently send students the message that we are looking for confirmation of what we already know rather than discussion of questions for which we have not yet found answers. Students can have a huge impact on the quality of the educational experience of the school community, including both peers and teachers. With the sense of agency that students feel when teacher leaders work in partnership with them also comes a sense of responsibility to create a high-quality school community.

ASSESSMENTS THAT HELP AND ENCOURAGE STUDENTS

The continual exchange of information between students and teachers in the classroom and in the school as a whole can generate trust and a sense of belonging. This is possible when it's clear that the purpose of assessment is not to sort students but to ensure each one experiences success. In the classic words of Moffett and Wagner (1992), "Let all parties know that all activities are assessed all the time, but don't ever give the impression that the assessment is intended for anything but help and encouragement" (p. 246).

The ways in which we assess student learning have enormous potential to go far beyond simply telling us what students have learned; the assessments themselves can feed into a renewal of instruction and student learning. From projects and performances to conversations about daily progress, the full range of classroom assessment provides teacher leaders with insight into how to support and encourage student learning when the purpose of assessment is primarily formative rather than summative. Stated another way, "while frequent, specific feedback is essential to the student's progress all the time, the only point at which it makes sense to express the student's achievement as a grade is at the end of a marking period" (Miller, 2021, p. 98). As discussed in chapter 3 (page 43) in the context of designing action research, experts such as Vicki Spandel (Peha, 2018) and Susan Brookhart (2013) acknowledge that even summative assessment rubrics are most valuable when used to provide formative feedback to students while a project is in progress.

This section focuses on six assessment strategies that are flexible and easy to use often as part of the classroom routine.

1. Teacher observation and read-back of student activities

2. Sampling of class responses to an activity

3. Preference surveys

4. Progress logs

5. Student self-assessment and reflection

6. Student-teacher and peer conferences

Teacher Observation and Read-Back of Student Activities

As students engage in collaborative work, it would be wonderful if you could sit in with each group for the entire discussion, but that's not humanly possible. A teacher leader who is curious about how students are able to apply what they're learning can circulate through the classroom with a notebook and pencil, a tablet, or a laptop cart and write or type verbatim as much as they can catch of what students say. Don't worry about getting everything. What you're looking for is a meaningful sample, not a transcript. Halfway through the session, read some of the comments out loud and ask students to set goals for the second half. Those goals could include speaking up more if they haven't said much yet, backing up opinions with details, letting the conversation evolve naturally, and staying focused on whatever topic, goal, or essential question they have chosen or been invited to discuss. The samples you've jotted or typed may indicate new learning, misconceptions that need to be cleared up, insights that hadn't yet occurred to you, and areas for further exploration. At the very least, read-back lets students hear themselves and provides clear evidence that you care about them and their ideas.

Sampling of Class Responses to an Activity

Following a class activity, you can ask students to write for a few minutes: *What did you do? How did it go? What would you change? What's next?* Then ask them to underline just one key sentence, and go quickly around the class, giving everyone a chance to read that sentence out loud. The read-around provides both students and teacher with a quick glimpse at the activity's impact on the class as a whole. And the read-around may offer additional insights into the perspectives of individual students and how you might further connect with the students. Let's say students have been reading *The Great Gatsby* (Fitzgerald, 1925/2019) and have reached the moment when Nick Carraway looks out the window and comments, "I was within and without, simultaneously enchanted and repelled by the inexhaustible variety of life" (p. 24).

You've invited them to respond to that passage and then select just one line of their writing to read out loud. What students choose to share is likely to range from a restatement of Nick's thought to a description of a time when the student felt the same way to a nod to the sense of anomie that was rampant during the 1920s, when the book was written. These glimpses help you get to know students, and they help students get to know each other, building a collaborative culture within the class.

Preference Surveys

People like to be consulted about their preferences, from whom they'd like to represent them in their government to what they'd like to have for lunch. You can create opportunities throughout the year to consult students about their preferences, both in and out of the classroom. Students' responses may surprise you, and they will certainly help you make planning decisions that closely align with student needs and wishes. Providing students with opportunities to say what they prefer is not just being nice. As discussed in the Student Feedback section (page 70), giving students agency and voice and considering their feedback make a huge difference for their well-being, improve your practice, and increase the likelihood that they will speak up for themselves when that really matters. Figure 4.5 provides an example of a preference survey.

Check your preferences.

Do you prefer:
- ☐ Having your own desk and chair?
- ☐ Sitting at a table with others?

Do you prefer:
- ☐ Reading in a chair?
- ☐ Reading stretched out on the floor?

Do you prefer:
- ☐ Writing with a pencil?
- ☐ Writing with a pen?

Do you prefer:
- ☐ Mathematics facts?
- ☐ Mathematics word problems?

FIGURE 4.5: Preference survey.

*Visit **go.SolutionTree.com/teacherefficacy** for a free reproducible version of this figure.*

Progress Logs

Each student has unique strengths and needs, but you may notice a few learning goals seem to be especially challenging for many students. For example, my ninth graders tended to have a hard time with following formal source citation, reading out loud with expression, proofreading their own writing, and rotating roles during group work. Tracking progress on just a few troublesome goals helped me focus on these areas, follow up with individual students, and notice improvement or continued issues. Similar to the process checklists described in chapter 3 (page 43), which help students keep track of their progress in completing an assignment, progress logs are useful for formative assessment and feedback rather than grade generation. As students work on written assignments, performance tasks, and collaborative projects, you can observe, ask questions, and make quick notes in progress logs like the sample in figure 4.6.

Learning goal	September	October	November	December
Cite sources correctly.				
Read out loud with expression.				
Proofread written work.				
Contribute to group work.				

FIGURE 4.6: Sample progress log.

The log serves as a data bank where you can store anecdotal information and, over time, gain insight into how instruction can be aligned with students' needs and progress.

Student Self-Assessment and Reflection

Much like how to teach reading, how to approach assessing students can cause a debate that divides educators into two separate camps: (1) teacher as authority figure and (2) teacher as guide. But this is a false and distracting dichotomy. Teachers can and should be both authority figures and guides. Students need opportunities to develop self-knowledge and actively participate in their own educational experience, but they also have much to learn from teachers. In his post on the AllThingsAssessment blog titled "Six Myths of Summative Assessment," Tom Schimmer (2021) teases out the fine points:

> Students should definitely be brought inside the process of grade determination; even asked to participate and understand how evidence is synthesized. . . . This does not have to be a zero-sum game; more student involvement need not lead to less teacher involvement. This is about expansion within the process to include students along every step of the way; however, our training, expertise, and experience matter in terms of accurately determining student proficiency.

Although you will ultimately determine students' grades, it's important and meaningful to ask students to self-assess their work before they turn it in; this underscores the idea that evaluation should be a collaborative process. Since you are likely to spend far more time providing formative feedback (which should not include grades) than determining grades, you can say you respond to student work rather than grade the work, so the emphasis is on feedback and opportunities for improvement.

Some learning goals are specific to a particular subject area, grade level, or project, but others are more broadly applicable—for example, learning goals for collaboration, performance, and self-direction. In areas such as these, the goals remain the same. What changes are the nuances of students' understanding of the goals and students' sophistication in meeting them. Students' reflections on their work over time serve as rich sources of detail and insight for the teacher. Figure 4.7 (page 78) offers an example of a self-assessment and reflection form for students.

Student-Teacher and Peer Conferences

Another way to find out how a student is doing is to ask. Students of all ages are remarkably aware of their strengths and needs and tend to be straightforward and accurate about how they're doing. Student-teacher conferences can focus on a particular assignment, a subject area, a social concern, or a look at the larger picture. You and the student can work together to make a plan, determine next steps, and decide when and how to follow up. Educational consultant and former teacher Damian Cooper (2022) demonstrates the power of formative assessment that includes student-teacher conferences or conversations in his book *Rebooting Assessment*. The key is to differentiate for individual students based on the gaps that teachers can identify by talking to them. As Cooper (2022) puts it in describing his assessment of the learning of science fair participants, "Only by engaging these budding scientists in conversation was I able to get beyond the sometimes superficial evidence of learning reflected in the products they displayed" (p. 43).

You will probably meet some of these goals through the natural give-and-take of collaboration. But some goals will require conscious thought and effort. In the Comments column, leave a note to yourself about each goal. How are you doing? What have you tried? What would you do differently next time? Give yourself credit for what you're doing well, and look for things you'd like to do better.

Collaboration learning goals	Comments
Act responsibly with the interests of the larger community in mind.	
Deal positively with praise, setbacks, and criticism.	
Demonstrate the ability to work effectively with diverse teams.	
Be open and responsive to new and diverse perspectives; incorporate group input and feedback.	
Exercise flexibility and willingness to be helpful in making necessary compromises to accomplish a common goal.	
Set and meet high standards and goals for delivering quality work on time.	
Assume shared responsibility for collaborative work.	
Adapt to varied roles and responsibilities.	

Source: Miller, 2021, p. 17; adapted from Partnership for 21st Century Learning, 2019.

FIGURE 4.7: Chart for self-assessment and reflection on collaboration.

*Visit **go.SolutionTree.com/teacherefficacy** for a free reproducible version of this figure.*

In addition to making time for student-teacher conferences, set aside time for peer conferences for every major assignment. Students become aware of how they are doing and accurate in their self-assessment when they have regular opportunities to talk through their works in progress, just as such opportunities to talk through lesson plans help teachers. These conferences can also help students broaden their thinking about what is possible and see the range of approaches taken by other students. When teachers model these assessment-focused conferences, they help students practice metacognitive and assessment skills they need to develop to get the most out of peer conferences (Cooper, 2022).

These classroom assessment strategies are intended not to produce grades but to increase your knowledge of students and to help and encourage students as they engage in learning. Taking a positive approach to teaching and learning and getting to know students well make it easier to figure out how to handle problems when they arise.

PROBLEM SOLVING

Responding to unexpected problems and challenges is part of being an educator of any role, but it's especially so for a teacher leader. Sometimes families expect more than teachers can provide. Sometimes a colleague doesn't come through for students or for the team. Sometimes students get in trouble. Human beings are not perfect. Yet we are very fond of being right. It's hard to keep lofty goals in mind when things get tense and we feel that someone else is to blame. When there is a problem to solve, the detailed and deep knowledge of students that a teacher leader gains by gathering and studying classroom data becomes an essential resource. The teacher leader can help all parties to the problem figure out how to move forward by focusing on solving the problem rather than determining who's right or who's to blame. The following are tips for moving toward a solution.

- Try to see beyond your expectations to what is really there.
- Acknowledge the problem without engaging in it.
- Listen and be sure you understand the facts.
- Try to build trust rather than assign blame.
- If the situation is tense, take a break, but schedule another meeting soon.
- Focus on finding a way to move forward rather than being right.
- If the situation remains tense, ask for help.

For example, a common school problem is plagiarism, which a student may do inadvertently or intentionally. It can take the form of copying someone else's homework or cutting and pasting someone else's work from a webpage. Students who know they are good people will excuse themselves for taking a shortcut that makes schoolwork a little less time consuming. And in a classroom where collaboration is encouraged, a student may have difficulty seeing the difference between material that is freely shared and material that requires acknowledgment.

As students get older, plagiarism can get them in increasingly serious trouble. To help students understand plagiarism and its consequences, your school district may have a policy that defines plagiarism and states that it will not be tolerated. Yet strict rules can result in unintended consequences. What will help a student move forward may not align with policy. In one case, a student might most benefit from revising an assignment in consultation with the teacher so that any areas of confusion about academic integrity can be cleared up. In another situation, it might be time for a student to receive a zero and the unequivocal message that plagiarism has consequences, including notification of the student's family and a meeting with the teacher. Moments like these are difficult for everyone involved. The student and family tend to be upset with the teacher, and the teacher tends to feel defensive. Teacher leaders can serve as buffers by using the previously listed tips, supporting the teacher, and helping family members see the situation as an opportunity to help the student accept responsibility and make better decisions in the future.

SUMMARY

This chapter focused on the ways in which teacher leaders can have a direct hand in renewing and improving instruction and student learning through curriculum and assessment design. Curriculum and assessment can go from sources of stress to ways to empower your students, your practice, and the entire school.

The chapter closed by discussing how teacher leaders can spearhead problem solving within the school. Handled with compassion, problems can become opportunities for all parties to gain increased respect for one another and to develop the resilience everyone needs in order to respond to the inevitable challenges that life in a complicated world presents. In his book *Fearless Schools*, Douglas Reeves (2021) expresses this beautifully: "The relationships, challenges, love, and support of others are keys to resilience from all the setbacks that life gives us" (p. 70). Whether we're trying to solve a problem, putting in the time and effort to meet each student's needs, or providing feedback and follow-up on a teacher-generated curriculum, we teacher leaders thrive in a collaborative school community where opportunities to participate and contribute are, quite literally, endless.

CURRICULUM-WRITING GUIDELINES

Curriculum Guidelines (These guidelines can be used to evaluate a curriculum in progress.)	Alignment of Curriculum With Guidelines		
	Total	Partial	Not So Much
Select learning goals that are truly essential (right at the core of the grade level or content area).			
Limit the number of learning goals so each one can be woven throughout the curriculum, giving students many opportunities to practice and, over time, achieve enduring mastery of each goal.			
Students learn best when they feel known and have a sense of belonging. Make getting to know students' interests and needs a universal priority, and identify methods and materials in the curriculum that are relevant to students.			
Focus the curriculum not just on teaching but on helping students learn how to learn.			
Include performance assessments that invite students to demonstrate their mastery of learning goals. Students can demonstrate what they have achieved in many ways: a portfolio with reflective commentary, an account of the process of designing and completing a multistep project, and a wide variety of other projects and performances.			

NEXT STEPS FOR RENEWAL AND IMPROVEMENT OF INSTRUCTION AND STUDENT LEARNING

The following tool details some steps you can take to experiment with strategies for renewing and improving instruction and student learning. For each step, note the date you tried it and reflect on how it went. *What did you do? How did it go? What would you change? What's next?* There are spaces available at the end for you to plan additional steps you can take toward teacher leadership.

Next Steps Tried	Date Tried	Reflection
Consider your school or district process for updating curriculum. Identify one additional thing that you could contribute to this process.		
Experiment with asking your students for feedback on a major assignment, a unit of study, or your approach to teaching.		
Use student feedback to improve some aspect of an assignment, a unit, or instruction.		

Identify the strategies you use to get to know your students. Create an opportunity to exchange such strategies with a colleague.			

CONCLUSION

ADVOCATES IN THE CLASSROOM

As a teacher leader, you are in a position to influence how people think about what goes on in school. We know there can sometimes be problems with how the public perceives teachers and schools. Perception is reality until it's replaced with a better understanding of what teachers do, how schools work, and what impact all of this has on the students who will become the leaders, innovators, and entrepreneurs of the future. Advocation for student learning and the profession of teaching can take place outside the classroom, but it also happens every day inside the classroom as teacher leaders test materials and methods against the ultimate standard: Are they good for students? Everything a teacher does could be seen as a way of advocating for student learning and the profession—everything from improving instruction to bringing about better student outcomes, and from mentoring and motivating new teachers to connecting with families so they see how the teachers' work is preparing students for the future. From this perspective, every teacher leader is a classroom champion in both senses of the term: making the classroom an outstanding place for students to grow as individuals and championing each student's right to learn.

Teacher leaders have the best of two worlds, combining the challenges and joys of teaching with the problem solving and pleasures of making time for colleagues and the school community. Both in and out of the classroom, teacher leaders can help shift the emphasis from what is taught to what is learned (DuFour & Fullan, 2013), mindful of the impact that student learning can have on an individual's life and on the lives of all who come in contact with that individual over a lifetime. Advocating for student learning and the teaching profession is time well spent. It makes a significant contribution to the larger community—one that is potentially life altering for students.

As I studied peer reviewers' comments on the first draft of this book, it struck me that one of the reviewers identified specifically as a teacher leader. The other reviewers mentioned a content area, a grade level, or a specific role such as instructional coach.

What they had to say suggested that all six of them played leadership roles. The one who did identify as a teacher leader put it in words that kept me going as I worked on this book:

> Many books are written about leadership, and usually, the audience is school or district administrators. To actually write a book designated about teacher leadership is important to support and validate the work being done in so many school communities by teachers who are leading from their classroom. (J. Josaphat, personal communication, June 11, 2022)

Teachers who lead from the classroom are an underreported but essential force in making schools work for students, colleagues, and families. Louis S. Nadelson, Loi Booher, and Michael Turley (2020) from the Department of Leadership Studies in the University of Central Arkansas's College of Education have studied the degree to which classroom teachers identify themselves as leaders. The premise that inspired the study is significant: "Teachers must identify as leaders to effectively navigate the challenges of teaching and learning" (Nadelson et al., 2020). What these researchers have found is that most teachers see themselves primarily as "conveyers of knowledge" (Nadelson et al., 2020). Teachers might acknowledge the importance of leadership from the classroom yet not perceive leadership as equal in importance to their teaching practice.

Every teacher who gets to know each student's unique combination of strengths, interests, and needs and builds on that knowledge to help each student learn is a leader whose example and encouragement change lives. Yet there is another dimension of teacher leadership to be found in teachers who identify as teacher leaders, activating leadership from the classroom that exerts influence and impact both in and out of the classroom. Those who serve as teacher leaders have the potential to sustain a movement of immense consequence to education through collaboration, innovation, research, outreach to the community, and advocacy for student learning and the profession of teaching. Key to the continued development of this movement is teachers' perceiving and identifying themselves as teacher leaders, emphasizing that dual role to underscore the equal importance of teaching and leading.

REFERENCES AND RESOURCES

Abitabile, A. W. (2020, January). How school leadership affects teacher retention. *Principal Leadership*, *20*. Accessed at www.nassp.org/publication/principal-leadership /volume-20/principal-leadership-january-2020/making-teachers-stick-january-2020 on November 30, 2022.

Ayres, A. T. (2022, May 17). *3 tips for partnering with parents for student success*. Accessed at www.edutopia.org/article/3-tips-partnering-parents-student-success on June 7, 2022.

Azorín, C., & Fullan, M. (2022). Leading new, deeper forms of collaborative cultures: Questions and pathways. *Journal of Educational Change*, *23*(3–4), 131–143. Accessed at https://link.springer.com/article/10.1007/s10833-021-09448-w on November 17, 2022.

Bagley, S. S. (2016, February 15). Teacher leaders or teacher-leaders? An argument on behalf of hyphenated hybridity. *Teachers College Record*. Accessed at https://education .uw.edu/sites/default/files/1279/Teacher%20Leaders%20or%20Teacher-Leaders.pdf on July 31, 2022.

Barger, M. M., Kim, E. M., Kuncel, N. R., & Pomerantz, E. M. (2019). The relation between parents' involvement in children's schooling and children's adjustment: A meta-analysis. *Psychological Bulletin*, *145*(9). Accessed at https://pubmed.ncbi.nlm .nih.gov/31305088 on October 25, 2022.

Barile, N. (n.d.). *Top 10 free lesson-planning resources for teachers*. Accessed at www.wgu .edu/heyteach/article/top-10-free-lesson-planning-resources-teachers1809.html on October 27, 2022.

Bogenschneider, K., & Johnson, C. (2004, February). *Family involvement in education: How important is it? What can legislators do?* West Lafayette, IN: Policy Institute for Family Impact Seminars. Accessed at www.purdue.edu/hhs/hdfs/fii/wp-content /uploads/2015/06/fia_brchapter_20c02.pdf on April 7, 2022.

Brookhart, S. M. (2013). *How to create and use rubrics for formative assessment and grading*. Alexandria, VA: ASCD.

Calkins, L. (2000). *The art of teaching reading*. Hoboken, NJ: Prentice Hall.

Calkins, L. (2015). *Units of study for teaching reading*. Portsmouth, NH: Heinemann.

Calkins, L. (2023). *Units of study in reading*. Portsmouth, NH: Heinemann.

Chalk. (2021, November 17). *What are essential questions? Explained by experts*. Accessed at www.chalk.com/resources/essential-questions on November 1, 2022.

Colburn, L., & Beggs, L. (2020). *The wraparound guide: How to gather student voice, build community partnerships, and cultivate hope*. Bloomington, IN: Solution Tree Press.

Cooper, D. (2022). *Rebooting assessment: A practical guide for balancing conversations, performances, and products*. Bloomington, IN: Solution Tree Press.

Cox, J. W., Rich, S., Chiu, A., Thacker, H., Chong, L., Muyskens, J., & Ulmanu, M. (2022, November 22). More than 323,000 students have experienced gun violence at school since Columbine. *The Washington Post*. Accessed at www.washingtonpost.com /graphics/2018/local/school-shootings-database on November 22, 2022.

Cushman, K. (1989, December 12). Asking the essential questions: Curriculum development. *Horace*, 5(5). Accessed at http://essentialschools.org/horace-issues /asking-the-essential-questions-curriculum-development on August 30, 2009.

Darling-Hammond, L., & Cook-Harvey, C. M. (2018, September). *Educating the whole child: Improving school climate to support student success*. Palo Alto, CA: Learning Policy Institute. Accessed at https://learningpolicyinstitute.org/sites/default/files/product -files/Educating_Whole_Child_REPORT.pdf on November 17, 2022.

Depka, E. (2022). *The authentic standards-based environment: A systematic approach to learning targets, assessment, and data*. Bloomington, IN: Solution Tree Press.

DuFour, R. (2004). What is a "professional learning community"? *Educational Leadership*, 61(8), 6–11. Accessed at www.allthingsplc.info/files/uploads/DuFourWhatIsA ProfessionalLearningCommunity.pdf on March 27, 2022.

DuFour, R., & Fullan, M. (2013). *Cultures built to last: Systemic PLCs at Work*. Bloomington, IN: Solution Tree Press.

DuFour, R., DuFour, R., Eaker, R., Many, T. W., & Mattos, M. (2016). *Learning by doing: A handbook for Professional Learning Communities at Work* (3rd ed.). Bloomington, IN: Solution Tree Press.

Fitzgerald, F. S. (2019). *The great Gatsby*. Knoxville, TN: Wordsworth Classics. (Original work published 1925)

Fredricks, J. A., Blumenfeld, P. C., & Paris, A. H. (2004). School engagement: Potential of the concept, state of the evidence. *Review of Educational Research*, 74(1), 59–109.

Gates, S. (2018, October 18). *Benefits of collaboration*. Accessed at www.nea.org /professional-excellence/student-engagement/tools-tips/benefits-collaboration on June 18, 2022.

Global Family Research Project. (2018a, October). *Joining together to create a bold vision for next-generation family engagement: Engaging families to transform education*. New York: Carnegie Corporation of New York. Accessed at https://globalfrp.org/content /download/419/3823/file/GFRP_Family%20Engagement%20Carnegie%20Report .pdf on November 23, 2022.

Global Family Research Project. (2018b, October). *Joining together to create a bold vision for next-generation family engagement: Engaging families to transform education* (Executive summary). Accessed at https://globalfrp.org/content/download/421/3844/file/GFRP _ExecutiveSummary.pdf on January 9, 2023.

Glossary of Education Reform. (2014, December 1). *Teacher-leader*. Accessed at www.ed glossary.org/teacher-leader on March 31, 2022.

Glossary of Education Reform. (2015, May 14). *Action research*. Accessed at www.ed glossary.org/action-research on November 23, 2022.

Goldstein, D. (2022, May 22). In the fight over how to teach reading, this guru makes a major retreat. *The New York Times*. Accessed at www.nytimes.com/2022/05/22/us /reading-teaching-curriculum-phonics.html on June 17, 2022.

Gonzalez, J. (2013, October 13). *Open your door: Why we need to see each other teach* [Blog post]. Accessed at www.cultofpedagogy.com/open-your-door on November 1, 2022.

Israel, M. (n.d.). *Teachers observing teachers: A professional development tool for every school.* Accessed at www.educationworld.com/a_admin/admin/admin297.shtml on December 5, 2022.

Lalor, A. D. L. (2022, July 27). *5 elements of a relevant curriculum*. Accessed at www1.ascd .org/el/articles/5-elements-of-a-relevant-curriculum on July 29, 2022.

Lesnick, L. (n.d.). *Where the heart is: 7 books about home for kids*. Accessed at www.read brightly.com/kids-books-about-home on July 31, 2022.

Marzano, R. J., Warrick, P. B., Rains, C. L., & DuFour, R. (2018). *Leading a High Reliability School*. Bloomington, IN: Solution Tree Press.

McKenzie, J. (2016, October). Essential questions vs. questions of import. *The Question Mark, 13*(1). Accessed at http://questioning.org/oct2016/essentialQ.html on November 1, 2022.

Meeting. (n.d.). In *Cambridge dictionary*. Accessed at https://dictionary.cambridge.org/us /dictionary/english/meeting on September 2, 2022.

Miller, J. J. (2021). *The student-centered classroom: Transforming your teaching and grading practices*. Bloomington, IN: Solution Tree Press.

Moffett, J., & Wagner, B. J. (1992). *Student-centered language arts, K–12*. Portsmouth, NH: Boynton/Cook.

Nadelson, L. S., Booher, L., & Turley, M. (2020). Leaders in the classroom: Using teaching as a context for measuring leader identity. *Frontiers in Education*, *5*(525630). Accessed at www.frontiersin.org/articles/10.3389/feduc.2020.525630/full on June 19, 2022.

National Association of State Directors of Teacher Education and Certification. (2021). *Model code of ethics for educators*. Washington, DC: Author. Accessed at www.nasdtec .net/page/MCEE_Doc on June 19, 2022.

National Council on Teacher Quality. (2019). *State of the states 2019: Teacher and principal evaluation policy*. Washington, DC: Author. Accessed at www.nctq.org/pages/State-of -the-States-2019:-Teacher-and-Principal-Evaluation-Policy on June 19, 2022.

National Education Association. (2020, July). *The teacher leader model standards*. Accessed at www.nea.org/resource-library/teacher-leader-model-standards on January 24, 2022.

Olson, A. L., & Peterson, R. L. (2015, April). *Student engagement: Strategy brief*. Lincoln, NE: Student Engagement Project, University of Nebraska–Lincoln. Accessed at https://k12engagement.unl.edu/strategy-briefs/Student%20Engagement%20 11-10-15%20.pdf on October 23, 2022.

Partnership for 21st Century Learning. (2019). *Framework for 21st Century Learning definitions*. Accessed at http://static.battelleforkids.org/documents/p21/P21 _Framework_DefinitionsBFK.pdf on September 9, 2022.

Peha, S. (2018, April 11). *An interview with Vicki Spandel, developer of the Six Trait Writing Model*. Accessed at https://medium.com/@stevepeha/an-interview-with-vicki-spandel -developer-of-the-six-trait-writing-model-af29a7400610 on October 29, 2022.

Perry, T. (2022, June 8). *Promoting student-led learning in elementary school*. Accessed at www.edutopia.org/article/promoting-student-led-learning-elementary-school on June 26, 2022.

Reeping, P. M., Gobaud, A. N., Branas, C. C., & Rajan, S. (2021). K–12 school shootings: Implications for policy, prevention, and child well-being. *Pediatric Clinics of North America*, *68*(2), 413–426. Accessed at https://pubmed.ncbi.nlm.nih.gov /33678295 on October 25, 2022.

Reeves, D. (2021). *Fearless schools: Building trust and resilience for learning, teaching, and leading*. Boston: Creative Leadership Press.

Schimmer, T. (2021, December 13). *Six myths of summative assessment* [Blog post]. Accessed at https://allthingsassessment.info/2021/12/13/six-myths-of-summative -assessment on December 5, 2022.

Schimmer, T., Hillman, G., & Stalets, M. (2018). *Standards-based learning in action: Moving from theory to practice*. Bloomington, IN: Solution Tree Press.

Schleifer, D., Rinehart, C., & Yanisch, T. (2017). *Teacher collaboration in perspective: A guide to research*. New York: Public Agenda. Accessed at https://files.eric.ed.gov/fulltext/ED591332.pdf on June 18, 2022.

Schmoker, M. (2021, May 1). *The obvious path to better professional development*. Accessed at www.ascd.org/el/articles/the-obvious-path-to-better-professional-development on March 20, 2022.

Skinner, E., Furrer, C., Marchand, G., & Kindermann, T. (2008). Engagement and disaffection in the classroom: Part of a larger motivational dynamic? *Journal of Educational Psychology, 100*(4), 765–781.

Stahnke, R., & Blömeke, S. (2021). Novice and expert teachers' situation-specific skills regarding classroom management: What do they perceive, interpret and suggest? *Teaching and Teacher Education, 98*, 103243.

Surr, W., Zeiser, K. L., Briggs, O., & Kendziora, K. (2018, October). *Learning with others: A study exploring the relationship between collaboration, personalization, and equity*. Washington, DC: American Institutes for Research. Accessed at https://jfforg-prod-new.s3.amazonaws.com/media/documents/18-5487_AIR_Learning_with_Others_EXT_Final_Report_10518_links_Final.pdf on November 17, 2022.

Terada, Y. (2021, August 13). *How novice and expert teachers approach classroom management differently*. Accessed at www.edutopia.org/article/how-novice-and-expert-teachers-approach-classroom-management-differently on October 24, 2022.

Terada, Y., & Merrill, S. (2022, March 25). *The research on life-changing teaching*. Accessed at www.edutopia.org/article/research-life-changing-teaching on March 29, 2022.

Trinkle, C. (2018). *What's behind the revolving door: A study of push and pull factors influencing teacher retention* [Doctoral dissertation, Ball State University]. ProQuest. www.proquest.com/docview/2311958416/8155C3A0CD8449D4PQ/1

Trinkle, C. (2019, December). *With peer visits, teachers see for themselves how to improve practice*. Accessed at https://learningforward.org/wp-content/uploads/2019/12/With-peer-visits.pdf on November 1, 2022.

Tubach, T. (2022, June 15). *Using PBL to teach about homelessness*. Accessed at www.edutopia.org/article/using-pbl-teach-about-homelessness on June 26, 2022.

Tutt, P. (2022, February 4). *How to lead with empathy*. Accessed at www.edutopia.org/article/how-lead-empathy on March 8, 2022.

Vangrieken, K., Dochy, F., Raes, E., & Kyndt, E. (2015, April). Teacher collaboration: A systematic review. *Educational Research Review, 15*. Accessed at www.researchgate.net/publication/275723807_Teacher_collaboration_A_systematic_review on November 30, 2022.

Visible Learning. (2018). *Hattie ranking: 252 influences and effect sizes related to student achievement.* Accessed at https://visible-learning.org/hattie-ranking-influences-effect-sizes-learning-achievement on October 22, 2022.

Walker, T. (2022, February 1). *Survey: Alarming number of educators may soon leave the profession.* Accessed at www.nea.org/advocating-for-change/new-from-nea/survey-alarming-number-educators-may-soon-leave-profession on February 24, 2022.

Wiggins, G., & McTighe, J. (1998). *Understanding by design.* Alexandria, VA: ASCD.

Zmuda, A., Tomaino, M., & Miller, J. J. (2001). *High stakes high school: A guide for the perplexed parent.* New York: Simon & Schuster.

INDEX

A

action research
    about, 43–44
    classroom action research, steps for,
      44–53
    demonstration lessons and, 54–57
    reproducibles for, 59–60
    summary, 57–58
    teacher leader responsibilities and, 6
activism and teacher leader responsibilities,
    8, 9–10
Alberino, C., 55
assessments
    about, 73–74
    preference surveys and, 75
    progress logs and, 76
    sampling of class responses to an
      activity, 74–75
    self-assessment and reflection on
      collaboration, chart for, 78
    self-assessment and reflection,
      student, 76–77
    self-assessment, sample chart of, 54
    student-teacher and peer conferences
      and, 77–78
    teacher observation and read-back of
      student activities, 74
Ayres, A., 37

B

back-to-school handouts, sample chart of
    topics included in, 36
Bagley, S., 1–2
behavior and classroom management,
26–27
Bogenschneider, K., 33
Booher, L., 86
Brookhart, S., 47–48

C

classroom action research. *See also*
  action research
    about, 44–45
      collecting information and
        developing a plan, 45–48
      implementing the plan and
        evaluating the results, 48–51
      repeating the process, 51–53
      teacher leader responsibilities and, 6
classroom collaboration. *See* collaboration
classroom visits, 68, 70
closer look at teacher leadership. *See*
  teacher leaders/teacher leadership
collaboration
    about, 16–20
    collaborative meetings and, 28–30
    congeniality and, 18
    formal evaluations and, 24, 26–27
    stress and burnout and, 20–24
    teacher-student dynamics and, 27–28
collaborative and connected culture. *See*
  culture
collaborative meetings, 28–30
collective teacher efficacy, 17
conferences, student-teacher and peer,
  77–78
Cooper, D., 77
culture

about, 15–16
classroom collaboration and, 16–30
connected school community and,
    30–38
reproducibles for, 39–41
summary, 38
curriculum
    about, 62
    aligning with vision, mission, and
        relevancy, 65
    curriculum-writing guidelines, 64–65
    elements of an effective curriculum,
        62–68
    follow-up and, 68, 70
    guaranteed and viable curriculum, 65
    reproducibles for, 81
    sample unit-of-study chart, 69
    student feedback and, 70–71, 73
    template for charting a unit of
        study, 67
Cushman, K., 64

E

effect size, 17
efficacy, 17
engagement
    stress and burnout and, 23
    teacher leader responsibilities and, 9
essential questions, 63–64
evaluations, 24, 26–27

F

families and connected school
    communities, 33–38. *See also*
    relationships
Fearless Schools (Reeves), 80
feedback
    assessments and, 73
    collaborative climate and, 26
    state-of-the-student report and, 71
    student feedback, 70–73
    teacher leader responsibilities and, 8
    using sample rubrics for image
        projects and, 51
formal evaluations, 24, 26–27

formative assessments, 76, 77. *See
    also* assessments

G

Gates, S., 16
Global Family Research Project, 33, 34, 35
Goldstein, D., 18, 19
Gonzalez, J., 55, 57–58, 69
guaranteed and viable curriculum, 65. *See
    also* curriculum

H

*How to Create and Use Rubrics for
    Formative Assessment and Grading*
    (Brookhart), 47

I

image projects, 49–51
introduction, 1–4

J

Johnson, C., 33

L

lesson planning. *See also* curriculum;
    schoolwide planning
        reproducibles for, 39
        sample lesson-planning chart, 25
lifelong learning and teacher leader
    responsibilities, 9

M

McKenzie, J., 63
meetings, 28–30
Moffett, J., 73

N

Nadelson, L., 86

O

observations
    classroom visits and, 68, 70
    teacher observation and read-back of

student activities, 74
"Obvious Path to Better Professional
    Development, The" (Schmoker), 61
online resources for educators, 46–47
"Open Your Door: Why We Need to See
    Each Other Teach" (Gonzalez), 55

P

peer conferences, 77–78
Perry, T., 7, 8
phonics, 18–19
problem solving, 79–80
process checklist, sample of, 52
progress logs, 76

R

read-back of student activities, 74
reading, approaches to, 18–19
Reeves, D., 20–21, 80
relationships
        behavior and classroom management
            and, 26–27
        connected school community and,
            30–38
        connections with families and, 33–38
        teacher-student dynamics and, 27–28
renewal and improvement of instruction
    and student learning
        about, 61–62
        assessments that help and encourage
            students and, 73–78
        problem solving and, 79–80
        reproducibles for, 81–83
        summary, 80
        teacher-written curriculum and,
            62–68, 70–71, 73
reproducibles
        for a closer look at teacher leadership,
            12–13
        for a collaborative and connected
            culture, 39–41
        for renewal and improvement of
            instruction and student learning,
            81–83

for research and professional learning
    to meet student needs, 59–60
research and professional learning to meet
    student needs. *See* action research
Rinehart, C., 16
rubrics
        collecting information and
            developing a plan for, 47–48
        implementing the plan and
            evaluating the results for, 48–51
        repeating the action research process,
            51–53
        sample rubric in progress, 53
        using sample rubrics for image
            projects, 50–51

S

sample lesson-planning chart, 25
Schleifer, D., 16
Schmoker, M., 61
school community
        about, 30
        connections with families, 33–38
        schoolwide planning and, 31–33
school culture. *See* culture
schoolwide planning, 31–33
scope-and-sequence approach, 62–63
self-assessment. *See also* assessments
        chart for self-assessment and
            reflection on collaboration, 78
        sample self-assessment chart, 54
        student self-assessment and
            reflection, 76–77
Socratic seminars, 7
Sparks, D., 55
standards-based approach, 62–63
stress and burnout, 20–24
student activities, 74–75
student feedback, 70–73. *See also* feedback
student-teacher conferences, 77–78
surveys
        assessments and, 74, 75
        sample room-preference survey, 32
        schoolwide planning and, 32–33
        survey of course preferences, 31

T

Teacher Collaboration in Perspective: A Guide to Research (Schleifer, Rinehart, and Yanisch), 16
teacher efficacy, 17
Teacher Leader Model Standards, 3
teacher leaders/teacher leadership
    about, 1–2, 5
    chart for rating alignment of teacher leader actions and your own practice, 10
    collaboration and, 19
    impact of, 85
    reproducibles for, 12–13
    responsibilities of, 5–6
    stress and burnout and, 22–23
    summary, 11
    teacher leaders in action, 6–10
teacher observation and read-back of student activities, 74

teacher-student dynamics, 27–28
teacher-written curriculum. *See* curriculum
teams and teacher leader responsibilities, 5
Trinkle, C., 54–55
Tubach, T., 7
Turley, M., 86

W

Wagner, B., 73
Walker, T., 20
whole-language approach to reaching reading, 18–19
"With Peer Visits, Teachers See for Themselves How to Improve Practice" (Trinkle), 54–55
Wraparound Services Center, 71

Y

Yanisch, T., 16

The Student-Centered Classroom

Jeanetta Jones Miller

Student-centered classrooms allow schools to fulfill their most enduring promise: to give students a fair chance to grow up literate, open-minded, and prepared to succeed. Begin making this critically important shift in your classroom with this resource as your guide.
BKF951

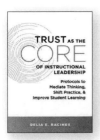

Trust as the Core of Instructional Leadership

Delia E. Racines

This go-to resource shares powerful, research-based protocols to support instructional leaders in building a community of trust. Gain inspired insights and actionable ideas for improving teaching and learning from educators who have done the work.
BKG047

Healthy Teachers, Happy Classrooms

Marcia L. Tate

Best-selling author Marcia L. Tate delivers 12 principles proven by brain research to help you thrive personally and professionally. Each chapter digs into the benefits of these self-care strategies and offers suggestions for bringing the practice to life in your classroom.
BKG044

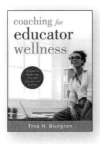

Coaching for Educator Wellness

Tina H. Boogren

Acquire evergreen coaching strategies alongside fresh new solutions for differentiating support for new and veteran teachers, addressing teacher self-care, and more. You'll turn to this resource again and again as you continue to improve your craft and help teachers find their own greatness.
BKF989

Solution Tree | Press

a division of

Solution Tree

Visit SolutionTree.com or call 800.733.6786 to order.

Quality team learning **from authors you trust**

Global PD Teams is the first-ever **online professional development resource designed to support your entire faculty on your learning journey.** This convenient tool offers daily access to videos, mini-courses, eBooks, articles, and more packed with insights and research-backed strategies you can use immediately.

GET STARTED
SolutionTree.com/**GlobalPDTeams**
800.733.6786